BEYOND
Affirmations

Empowering Black Women to Unlock Your Inner Power for Self-Love, Self-Worth, and Manifestation Mastery

J B Allen

BEYOND AFFIRMATIONS

Empowering Black Women to Unlock Your Inner Power for Self-Love, Self-Worth, and Manifestation Mastery

© All Rights Reserved. Copyright 2023 J B Allen

ALL RIGHTS RESERVED.

No part of this book or its associated ancillary materials may be reproduced or transmitted in any form or by any means, electronic or mechanical, including photocopying, recording, or by any information storage or retrieval system without permission of publisher.

Book design by Saqib_arshad

PRINTED IN THE UNITED STATES OF AMERICA | FIRST EDITION

Your FREE Gifts

As a way of saying *Thank You* for your purchase,
I'm offering you tons of goodies.

Scan me

Inside you will discover:

☑ 5 Essential Steps to take <u>*before*</u> creating your vision board. $9.97 value

☑ Unlock Your Dream Life: 7 Reflection Questions You Must Ask Yourself $14.97 value

☑ The Ultimate Planning Tool: 12-Month Goal Intention Cards $24.97 value

☑ Digital Vision Board Templates: Now you can carry your inspiration with you anytime, anywhere. $19.97 value

☑ 25 Additional Affirmation cards and Quotes $14.97 value

☑ 7 Simple Tips for Hosting a Mind-Blowing Vision Board Party! Priceless

$85 Value   FREE

Scan the QR Code if ~~you're ready~~ to design your dream life today!!

Contents

Introduction   1

CHAPTER 01: Manifesting Melanin Magic: Decoding the Power of Creation for Bold Black Women   7

CHAPTER 02: Affirmation Revelation: Unveiling the Power of Affirmations   27

CHAPTER 03: Slaying The Illusion: Liberating Black Women From Shallow Tactics With Unapologetic Brilliance   45

CHAPTER 04: Aligning with Your True Desires: The Blueprint for Rewriting Your Subconscious for Lasting Success   63

CHAPTER 05: Love Unleashed: The Empowered Equation for Self-Worth, Self-Love, and Your Inner Sparkle   81

CHAPTER 06: Desire on Point: Mastering the Art of Authentic Alignment with Precision and Purpose   95

CHAPTER 07: Visualize to Materialize: Unleashing Your Manifesting through the Art of Mental Mastery   107

CHAPTER 08: From Scarcity to Sisterhood: Embracing Abundance and Shattering Barriers as a Bold Black Woman   121

CHAPTER 09: Amplifying Manifestation Through Action   143

CHAPTER 10: Embracing Abundance, Gratitude, and Transforming Your Reality   159

CHAPTER 11: Positive Affirmations   177

Conclusion   195
Other Books by the author   201

Introduction

> "Knowledge by itself is not power, it's not enough. Rather, the true power lies in having the wisdom to apply knowledge effectively and appropriately."
>
> -UNKNOWN

The first step to changing any situation in life is to acknowledge there's something that needs changing, and then learning how to go about it.

If you're reading this, it's because you've realized you need a different way of approaching your life and mental growth. You've probably struggled and are still struggling with seeing yourself as worthy of your desires. There's still that little nagging voice in your head that tells you, you aren't. That voice naggingly lists the mistakes of your past and the possible failures of your future. You're unable to consistently stay motivated because it feels like you're swimming upstream, the journey is long and arduous forcing you to ask "what's the point?" The point is, when are you going to grab the steering wheel and take control? How can you win if you keep quitting the race? You are not alone

INTRODUCTION

These are familiar thoughts, not just for you, but also for me and many other Black women over the world.

We experience the common problems of putting our needs second to those of others. We are not groomed to see ourselves as worthy of respect and live the lives we truly desire.. We battle with the internal voices of our childhood, voices that have told us how we are supposed to live and who we are supposed to be for so long, that becoming who we truly want feels wrong. We struggle with treating ourselves with kindness and seeing ourselves with eyes of love because we've gotten so used to being picked apart.

That's why this book is so important. Especially at this turning point in your life.

Unlike every other thing you've read on manifestations, this book stands out by showing you exactly how to practice manifestations the right way to see the actual impact on your life. Here, you'll learn how to approach manifestations beyond words that you speak. You'll learn how to build the right mindset to attract your desires, how to set your intentions right, how to better listen to the universe/God/your higher power, and how to take the right steps towards the life you want.

So if you're reading this right now, I applaud you for your decision to break free. I applaud you for recognizing a problem in your life and picking up this book to help guide you on this new journey.

I decided to write this because at the start of my journey I tried looking for help. For someone who really understood me and would be able to help, but that was hard. I was the woman who couldn't look people in the eyes for fear of someone seeing what I really looked like. I was the woman stuck in a bad relationship because I was afraid to leave. What if I never found love again? Even though there was no real love and happiness where I was, how could I leave it? What if I wasn't one of those lucky women so loved by the universe and God that they find long lasting love and happiness? I was the woman always worrying about things never working out in my favor. I was the woman making all the moves (out of fear), then failing and believing I was cursed and hated by God. I was the woman hoping and dreaming of becoming but never was afraid to arrive because I kept settling for what I could get and listening to the voices that said I couldn't. I was the woman letting people walk over her and disrespect and disregard me because I didn't see myself as worthy. I was the woman who found it weird when other women had strong opinions and wild dreams and carried themselves mightily. For years I judged these women who had the life I admired and wanted for myself because why them and not me? I was the woman who couldn't see herself so any attention no matter how harmful, was welcomed.

I was that unhappy woman for so long.

But something happens when you decide it's enough and you need a new beginning. When you decide to stop being a victim to life and your past. When you want a real plan for your life.

It took me longer than needed to get the results I wanted, not because I wasn't trying. But because I had been following the superficial techniques I saw. The ones that told me to speak the life I wanted and watch it happen for me. Just like that. Imagine the consistent disappointments I dealt with on my journey. Speaking each day and seeing no change. Not until I realized what true manifestation was - not a

INTRODUCTION

magic wand but a perfect blend of affirmations, visualizations, and taking guided actions - did things start changing for me.

So I decided to write this book with all I learned to help other Black women master this journey of mental transformation the right way.

My journey wasn't easy - yours won't be too. Healing and growth is never linear. There are days you'll fall back or forget or simply not be in the mood. Whatever you feel on any given day throughout your journey, honor it. But get back up and continue moving forward.

That's what this book is going to help you with. In this book you'll learn practical steps to change the way you see and approach life by learning how to win the battle of the mind. This isn't like any other guide that just tells you how to think. This is a book tailored specifically to Black women and our struggles and experiences. You'll learn from examples of some other Black women how to master mental strength and transform your life. So you know you're not alone. You'll learn affirmations and lifestyle changes you can use to start trusting yourself more while following your divine guides so you can start rebuilding every area of your life. Some of the activities in this book may be difficult for you because they require pure honesty, but I beg you to do them. Think of yourself as a garden and the tough activities as pruning. The pruning is necessary for beautiful and healthy growth. By partaking in every exercise in this book, not only will you learn to better honor yourself and your dreams, you'll also learn the origins of your blocks and how to weaken their hold on you.

Regardless of where you are in your life now. Whether you're still young or older. Whether you're in an unhappy place or you've started on your way out of that unhappy place. Whether you have unfulfilled dreams or no dreams because you don't want to hurt yourself with hopes and dreams of better. I need you to know good is possible for you. And if you don't remember anything else, I need you to remember you are worthy. Of good, of love, of patience, of growth, of success, of people who see you, of praises and compliments, of being desired, of respect, of abundance, of anything your heart wants. No matter what you've heard and experienced at other times in your life. You are worthy.

As you start on this journey, the first thing I need you to do right now is tell yourself "I am worthy." Go ahead and say it. Write it somewhere you can always see it. Repeat it to yourself multiple times in the day. Set hourly reminders on your phone. Because the journey ahead is long and not easy, but you're worthy of seeing it through and reaching your destination.

Welcome to the beginning of the life you want.

Love,

Your motivating cheerleader

> "If you can think it, you can do it."
>
> — DIONNE WARWICK

Chapter 1

Manifesting Melanin Magic:
Decoding the Power of Creation for Bold Black Women

At first glance, this might seem like empty words of motivational speakers who encourage people to grasp at thin air. But that's so far from the truth. As much as you may want to doubt this, you are exactly what you think you are. Manifesting that melanin magic starts with boldness, hence the emphasis on being a bold Black woman. And now that you have that locked down, let's take a look at manifestation and how relevant it is in transforming your life.

Manifestation is powerful. It can give you that framework you need for intentional creation and manifesting your desired reality. This is the process of being intentional about attracting desired outcomes and experiences through focused thoughts. With this, you'll be harnessing the power of your positive energy and emotions to align with a specific reality.

To truly understand the power of manifestation in transforming your life, all you have to do is look at one of the most successful Black women of our time, Oprah Winfrey. Today, she is known as a renowned media mogul and amazing television host but that's not how it has always been. This amazing Black woman grew up in poverty and suffered sexual abuse which is more than enough to serve as a setback, especially for a woman of color looking to make it in the broadcast industry.

However, by her own admission, a key part of her success involved a lot of visualization and affirmation of her goals through the power of manifestation.

Here's some of her visualization techniques you can also practice :

- **Visualization.** Of course, there's no doubt that she's super talented. However, Oprah began visualizing her success and believing in her goals no matter how much it appeared that she was fighting an uphill battle. She believed and visualized what she wanted her life to look like and we have all witnessed the outcome. No doubt about it, Oprah continues to inspire millions of black women to believe in their dreams...that also means you.

- **Get clarity about what you want.** What is it that you truly want to achieve? How do you want to achieve this? When you carefully articulate and identify what you want and gain more clarity about setting your goals and achieving your desires, the next step is focusing your energy and attention on your desired outcome. So, when you think about it, it's all about having a greater sense of direction and purpose which manifestation contributes a lot to.

- **Positive Mindset.** We can't talk about the power of manifestation in transforming your life without emphasizing the impact of a positive mindset. Remember, you are what you think you are. Manifestation will never work alongside negative thoughts or emotions. You need to exude positive energy to attract the good things of life. Therefore, this emphasizes the importance of a positive belief system.

Encourage only empowering thoughts and affirmations. Make sure that these align with that outcome you desire and manifestation will work for you. When you shift your mindset from that of negativity, doubt and lack to one that embraces possibility and abundance, you can surely overcome those limiting beliefs holding you back and see life through a new lens of optimism.

Manifestation to transform your life also involves a lot of **self-reflection.** While on your manifestation journey, you have to embrace change that fosters your personal growth. During this journey, you may discover those patterns, fears and beliefs that have held you down for years and slowed down your progress. These limiting patterns would have kept you back from tapping into your true potential as a bold black woman. However, manifestation has one of the biggest advantages: *personal transformation.*

You'll come out of this renewed and with an increased level of self-awareness, and a good idea of your strengths and how to maximize them. This all keys into your ability to attract abundance and opportunities as manifestation works with the belief that you can make the universe work for you.

Career advancements, the relationship you believe you deserve, a better financial life…you can attract this from the universe (or God, Jehovah, Allah, your higher power, or whatever specific name you identify with) through manifestation. Attract this and take ownership of your life.

Manifestation is all about taking charge and being proactive. It encourages you to be resilient and recognize the true power you have to shape your life and achieve your deepest desires.

Here's a recap on how manifestation can help you:

- Encourage you to gain more clarity about setting your goals
- Work alongside a positive mindset
- Reveal things about yourself that you may not be happy to see - a step towards positive change

But, this strategy is not without its challenges.

As glamorous as it sounds, you need to be prepared for the challenges that you'll definitely face as a Black woman. Every Black woman's manifestation experience is different, as it is shaped by their lived experiences and unique intersectional identities. As Black women, we continue to face societal challenges and systemic barriers that have been in place for decades such as: classism, sexism, racism…you can't talk about your manifestation experience without exploring the impact of these as well.

In spite of these challenges, we can embrace the power of manifestation to challenge these societal norms and write our stories where we truly manifest our goals and dreams. So, what can influence your manifestation experience? Let's start with self-empowerment.

Self-empowerment

As mentioned earlier, a positive mindset is an important ingredient in this journey. You need to develop a strong sense of self-worth where you recognize your power as a Black woman and believe completely in your abilities. Here's one way it works, get a journal and write daily the different positive qualities you noticed about yourself for each day. Did you smile at a stranger today? Did you solve a complicated task at work? Navigate around a confrontational colleague? Reflecting on your day helps you see those typical actions that you would normally take for granted, but consistently rely on the fact that you're more amazing than you think.

You can manifest the resilience you need to face the various challenges that will come knocking when you hang on to your belief in your power and worth. This is relevant in all aspects of your life including relationships and career growth.

Embrace community

Another way to influence your manifestation experience is to embrace the importance of having a sense of community.

As Black women, the odds are strongly stacked against us. However, we can work together to manifest global positive change through the understanding that your individual success works better with the empowerment of the Black women community. Sharing this with you is one of the ways to foster the growth of our community of bold Black women.

Unfortunately, society through the media tries to promote the exact opposite. You're more likely to come across content on how Black successful women tear each other down instead of building each other up. It needs to stop because *"real queens fix each other's crowns, we don't try to remove them."* With our collective manifestation where we create safe spaces and make conscious efforts to support each other, you can have one of the best manifestation experiences ever.

You can use your manifestation experience to disrupt limiting stereotypes. To redefine what society considers impossible for us... To break those societal expectations that relegate Black women to the background. Your manifestation experiences can inspire and empower others like you, just like many Black women have done over time. Actively shape your reality through intentional thoughts and actions.

We can't explore manifestation journeys without talking about the intersectionality of race, gender and manifestation.

Intersectionality here seems like a big word. However, it simply means how various systems of oppression and social identities interact with each other to shape the unique challenges and experiences of people. What is the interaction between race, gender and manifestation? You can't begin a new journey without clearly highlighting those unique challenges that you'll encounter and how you can be successful in spite of them.

When we walk into a space, our skin is seen first, then our gender is seen first. But it doesn't stop there. There are so many layers to the Black woman's identity - light skinned vs. dark skinned... Christian vs. Muslim... Married vs. Single...Entrepreneur vs Executive.

We get caught up in that complex interplay of societal structures and power dynamics that can both destroy or help our manifestation experiences. Our challenges are distinct due to the relationship between sexism and racism. You can't control how much stereotypes, prejudice and systemic barriers you're exposed to in your manifestation journey but you can control how much it impacts your ability to manifest your desires.

The intersectionality of race and gender as regards manifestation can be seen in inequalities that reveal themselves as lack of representation, discrimination and limited access to resources which can all affect the amount of opportunities you can manifest. The double marginalization of sexism and racism can severely impact your experiences as a Black woman. More than a few of us have stories of how we've been sidelined, underestimated or overlooked in professional settings just because of this double marginalization. It's not unheard of to battle incidences of objectification and/or hypersexualization which can all affect self-worth and the belief in your goals and desires being achievable.

Despite these challenges, Black women have continued to break barriers and achieve their dreams. You can do the same/ Draw on the power of community and manifestation to redefine the life you want for yourself. Your manifestation experiences can involve creating opportunities for yourself and others, dismantling systemic inequalities holding Black women down and reshaping narratives. Intersectionality is a way to reevaluate what it means to manifest your dreams and desires.

And this is what it is all about. Discussing the intersectionality of race, gender and manifestation helps us shine light on the unique challenges of Black women. It also draws attention to our aspirations and where we draw strength from. When we understand these intersectional experiences, we can foster an environment that empowers you as you go on your manifestation journey.

The connection between thoughts, beliefs and reality

This relationship is an important foundation for manifestation. And that's why we need to examine each individually and then talk about the connection between them. Thoughts refer to the mental processes that include both subconscious and conscious thoughts. These play an important role in shaping our perception of reality. What's going on in your mind right now? Those are your thoughts. The power of your thoughts lies in how they can affect your mindset, and that's why you should only focus on positive thoughts especially in your manifestation journey.

Beliefs are not the same as thoughts. Beliefs are the deeply held convictions you have about yourself, others, your immediate environment and the world at large. Beliefs are what shape your actions and inactions, but there are lots of factors that influence what you eventually identify as your beliefs. These could be social conditioning, personal convictions and past experiences. Your beliefs can also serve as filters through which you interpret the opportunities that come your way. Beliefs shape thoughts.

However, not all beliefs foster progress. So, in the course of your manifestation journey, you have to identify those limiting beliefs that may stop you from manifesting your desires. A very common one with Black women is our belief about **money and success.**

Unfortunately, we're more often than not faced with the limiting belief that we're only allowed to have a certain amount of money due to our backgrounds or the systemic blockages that challenge us as Black women.

This is one of those beliefs you have to get rid of for your manifestation to yield positive results.

Finally, let's talk about reality. This is the experience or external circumstance that we eventually come in contact with in life. However, this is heavily influenced by our thoughts and beliefs. What you perceive as reality can be shaped by your thoughts and beliefs, so your reality of what you attract, the actions to take, what you repel and how you interpret events around you is a function of both your thoughts and beliefs.

So, this is the time to critically reflect on your thoughts and beliefs. Answer the following questions:

- What is your definition of success?
- How do you feel about money? How do you talk about money?
- Would you say you are successful financially? If not, what's stopping you?
- What's your view on romantic relationships?
- How do you know you're in a healthy relationship?

When you make conscious efforts to harness only thoughts and beliefs that are geared towards your desires, only then can you transform your reality for good. This is how you know that your thoughts, beliefs and reality are all connected.

So, how can you align your thoughts and beliefs with the reality you desire so you can truly harness the power of manifestation?

The first step is knowing how to manage your emotions. Our thoughts and beliefs are great influencers of our emotional state. To give you an idea of just how powerful emotions are, think about the last time you were really sad and disappointed and analyze the effect it has on your entire body. That sadness makes you feel actual physical aches, right? This lets you know just how much these powerful energy signals can help or destroy your manifestation process. Now try to do this in reverse. Think about the last time you experienced something that made you feel truly happy and satisfied and analyze how it makes you feel. Do you feel a sense of peace washing over you? That's a big difference. Now, reflect on how you feel most days, do you generally feel a sense of sadness or calm and happiness? What thoughts do you reflect on the most?

When you encourage empowering beliefs and positive thoughts, you'll mostly feel emotions such as peace, confidence, gratitude, optimism and joy. These are all amazing emotions that can elevate our vibrational frequency so much that we attract only positive experiences. But what happens when you dwell on mostly limiting beliefs and negative thoughts? The only emotions that will accompany these are terrible ones such as frustration, pessimism, self-doubt, anxiety and fear. These are all repellents to your desires for your life as a bold Black woman.

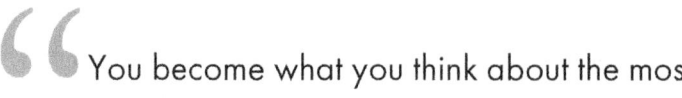

> You become what you think about the most."
>
> - UNKNOWN

Next, control what takes your attention and focus the most. What do you focus your energy on the most as you go about your daily life? Harnessing the power of manifestation means being disciplined with what takes your attention. When you draw more focus towards the positive situations you would like to manifest, you can consciously direct your thoughts towards achieving your goals. It's all about aligning your energy to the right channel. If you're having trouble with controlling what takes your attention, you need to spend some time practicing positive affirmations to strengthen your thoughts, beliefs and reality through intentional reprogramming. We'll get back to this again before the end of the chapter.

However, manifestation techniques like visualization and positive affirmations help to reinforce empowering thoughts and beliefs over time which is great for reconfiguring your subconscious into making positive thoughts a part of your being. It is important to uplift and center the achievements and experiences of bold Black women in our conversation on manifestation. So, what better way to do this than to explore the story of one of the best out there? Serena Williams!

Serena Williams is more than a tennis champion; she used her success to show Black women around the world that we can be ourselves and achieve greatness. Most importantly, she has mentioned in several interviews how the power of positive thinking and visualization has enhanced her performance and contributed greatly to the immense success she enjoys.

One time, she spoke a lot about how she envisions herself holding trophies, breaking records and winning her matches even before she steps on the court. This shows you the power of visualization, especially with how it helped to advance Serena's tennis career. Every day, she mentally rehearsed her success and stayed in control of her mind. With this, she maintained a winning mindset and was focused enough to achieve it.

Of course, this tennis star faced lots of challenges especially with difficult matches and unanticipated setbacks. She overcame them by maintaining a positive attitude, embracing a mindset of resilience and affirming her abilities with her unwavering belief in herself. Serena's approach to manifestation has always been level-headed and goal-oriented, and this is a template that can work for you too, especially when you incorporate affirmations into your daily life.

Affirmations as a powerful tool for manifestation

- I am capable of achieving my goals.
- I deserve success.
- I am worthy of love.

When was the last time you said something nice about yourself and really meant it? These are affirmations and they are often underestimated. In the manifestation process, positive affirmations can be very effective in aligning your thoughts and beliefs to attract your goals and desires. How much of your desires do you think you can attract if you consistently tell yourself that you're not good enough?

Well, the answer to that is none. Incorporating affirming statements like you deserve success and riches will reprogram your subconscious mind to let go of limiting beliefs and embrace empowering thoughts instead. A positive and supportive mindset goes a long way in making manifestation successful in your life. Your subconscious mind is responsible for a lot of automatic beliefs, thoughts and eventually reality that form a key part of your existence.

However, it operates based on what you feed it. When you continuously feed your subconscious with negative programming, it's going to shape the reality you think you deserve and definitely not a good one. However, when you feed it consistently and over a long time with positive programming, your thoughts, actions and reality are shaped towards the desires of a bold black woman. Still, this won't work if you don't address two specific issues: **your method of self-reflection and limiting beliefs.**

Manifestation will open your eyes and mind to a lot of things you may not be happy to know about yourself. This is the process of self-reflection where you seek to understand your true desires and gain more clarity about what resonates with your authentic self. It's not enough to just say you want to manifest wealth, does this align with your deeper purpose and fulfillment? Self-reflection is important to manifest desires that align with your true self. Still, this can be blocked by limiting beliefs.

Ask yourself the following questions to gain a deeper understanding of your subconscious beliefs:

- *Do you believe you deserve to be happy?*
- *What does happiness mean to you?*
- *What is blocking you from fully pursuing your happiness and success?*
- *How did your parents/guardians view/define success?*
- *What is their belief system around money?*

These are all roadblocks on the path to manifesting your desires and goals. Self-reflection and sometimes, therapy, can help you address these underlying issues. Yes, therapy is not exactly a favorite in traditional black communities as it has a history of being frowned on. However, this is emotional self care that can make a world of difference. Meanwhile, you should never underestimate the power of affirmations in helping you reprogram from these trauma and past experiences to take inspired outcomes that will give you the manifestation journey you deserve.

Manifestation cannot work without self-worth and self-love

Self-worth, self-love and empowerment are the foundation to the manifestation journey of bold black women. Do you believe that you deserve the outcomes and desires you want to manifest? This encompasses your self-worth. For us as Black women, we need to cultivate a strong sense of self-worth as we'll always be faced with systematic inequalities and societal barriers. While these keep rearing their ugly heads, you can cut them down by affirming and recognizing your inherent worthiness and right to achieve your dreams.

This works alongside the need to nurture self-love, that deep and unconditional love you have for YOU. And that means ALL OF YOU. Self-love doesn't discriminate. You embrace your strengths and weaknesses. You embrace everything that makes you uniquely you. Practicing self-love will help you build that resilience and confidence you need to manifest your desires successfully.

Take these action steps daily:

- Start your day with positive affirmations such as *"I am enough just as I am."*
- Take a few moments to reflect on the things in your life you are grateful for.

- Make time for activities that you enjoy at least twice a week. This can be indulging in a hobby or taking a relaxing bath.
- Always remember that saying no to friends and family is not a death sentence. Set healthy boundaries that show that your needs and well-being come first.
- You deserve kindness. So, anytime you make mistakes, remind yourself that you're not perfect and show compassion to yourself as much as you would do to someone special.

Finally, you have to recognize your power as a bold Black woman. Embrace it and know that you can create change in the trajectory of your life. Always remind yourself that you have the capacity to shape your life in line with your desires and that means embracing your authentic voice at all times. Take control of your life and destiny regardless of the negative societal narratives you may be surrounded with. This is how you break free from limitations and attain your true potential.

Never forget that self-worth, self-love and empowerment serve as foundational pillars for manifesting the true desires of your heart. Now that you know this, it's time to talk about how You may already be aware of how powerful affirmations are but how do they correlate to Alcoholics Anonymous? I'll meet you in the next chapter where it will be discussed.

Reflect and Empower: Understanding Manifestation and Its Impact:

SELF-REFLECTION QUESTIONS

What are the limiting beliefs I hold about myself as a Black woman?

....

....

....

....

....

....

....

What specific areas in my life do I struggle with feelings of unworthiness?

....

....

....

....

....

....

....

BEYOND AFFIRMATIONS

What specific challenges do I face as a black woman that can be addressed through positive affirmations?

....

....

....

....

....

What societal stereotypes influence my belief in my self-worth?

....

....

....

....

....

What empowering affirmations can I create to affirm my self-worth as a black woman?

....

....

....

....

....

What affirmations rooted in self-love and acceptance can help me fight limiting beliefs about my intelligence and beauty?

....

....

....

....

....

What fears and insecurities hold me back from fully embracing the power of affirmations in my life as a black woman?

....

....

....

....

....

How can affirmations help me heal from negative stereotypes or past traumas that have held me back?

....

....

....

....

....

BEYOND AFFIRMATIONS

Relationship between the way you think and the way you feel

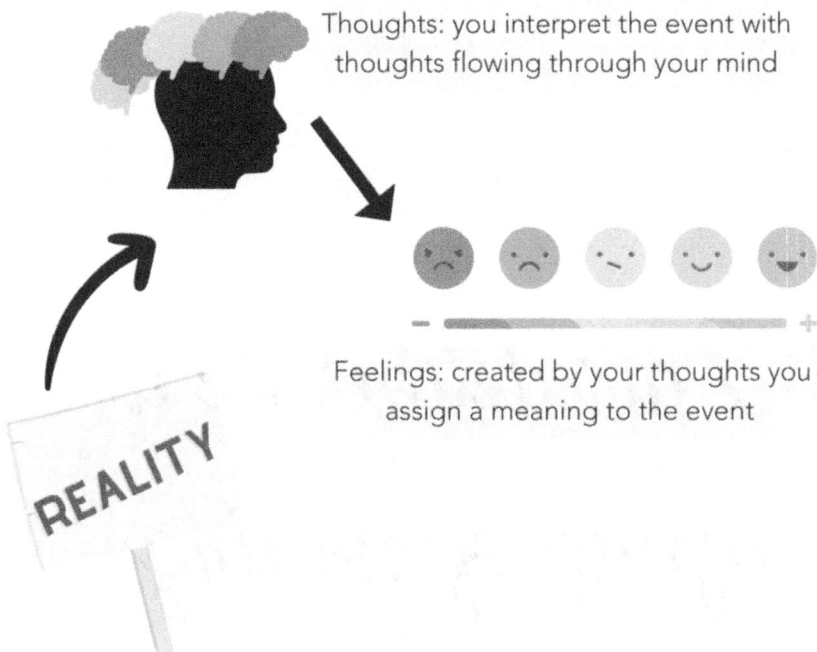

Thoughts: you interpret the event with thoughts flowing through your mind

Feelings: created by your thoughts you assign a meaning to the event

World: A series of negative, positive, neutral events

> "I am deliberate and afraid of nothing"
>
> — AUDRE LORDE

Chapter 2

Affirmation Revelation:
Unveiling the Power of Affirmations

Have you ever felt stuck in a negative feedback loop? Maybe you've struggled to see the positive in a situation, or you've felt overwhelmed with self-doubt and anxiety. Trust me, you're not alone.

We all have moments when our minds seem to be working against us. I have had negative waves of thoughts that pop up all the time: *"I'm not doing my best as a mom." "My financial status is not where I want it to be." "My friends are not as supportive as I would like"* and the list can go on and on if I let myself spiral. But, I don't.

What if I told you that a simple practice could help you break free from those thoughts and unlock your true potential?

When an alcoholic begins to spiral and needs professional help in a group setting, they attend AA (Alcoholics Anonymous) meetings. I'm not implying you are an alcoholic but, when your thoughts begin to spiral I want you also to have your own AA meeting. That stands for what I like to call *"Affirmations in Action."* In this chapter, we'll explore the power of Affirmations in Action and how they can transform your outlook on life. Get ready to unveil the incredible benefits of positive self-talk and discover a whole new way of thinking.

Affirmation Revelation: Unveiling the Power of Affirmations in Action

Positive Affirmations

Affirmations are precise statements you repeat or listen to until it is etched in your mind. Did you know that there's a difference between positive affirmations and negative? Some people think affirmations are fake and refuse to engage, but did you know that you affirm your beliefs daily whether you are aware of it or not? The real question is which affirmations do you speak daily, are they negative or positive?

When you say things like: "I'm not good at speaking in public," or "I'm never on time," or "I'm always gonna be fat, it's in my DNA." Those are negative affirmations. The more you speak to them, the more you make them a reality. You may not even be aware of what was affirmed to you as a child that you internalized. Were you constantly told things like: you're not a good test taker? You will never be great at math? Or, you don't live up to your potential? Or contrastingly, were you told: you are amazing at (insert subject/activity here)? Or, you will definitely excel in college? The belief systems we have about ourselves are things we were repeatedly told or affirmed in childhood. Those affirmations that we internalized can be both negative or positive. But there's usually never a balance, which ones tip your internal scale?

Positive affirmations are just as effective as negative ones. You still control the narrative, it just will take a conscious effort. So, take those negative affirmations and shift them into the positive in order to truly be the person you want to become. You will now say things like, "I am working daily at becoming a better public speaker," or "I am arriving at my destination 10 minutes early," or "I am exercising and being mindful of my health to reach my desired weight." Can you feel the difference? Positive affirmations are a great way to see yourself positively, and attract the world to you while you work on being the person you desire.

Whether you are speaking it in your heart or aloud, listening to it, or reading it from a written document, affirmations work when you stick with it.

"Words are powerful." It's a phrase we've all heard before, but have you ever considered the weight and impact our words have on our lives? Did you know that contrary to what numerous books have been telling you, affirmations alone cannot change your life. So yes, words are powerful but without some essential pieces, they'll just remain empty and dormant like a candle that hasn't been lit, incapable of giving you any true change. What are these pieces? Positive thinking and Action.

Affirmations are a tool used to shape and motivate the subconscious mind. They have become increasingly popular in mainstream culture. However, for the Black community, affirmations have been a long-standing tradition that dates back to our ancestors.

Affirmations, used in the form of daily mantras and positive self-talk, have been proven to have a profound effect on our mental and emotional well-being. Black people have endured centuries of systemic oppression, racism, and prejudice that have left deep scars on our collective psyche. Historically, affirmations have been a source of empowerment and strength for Black people as we navigated life's challenges, and they still hold immense cultural significance to this day. When verbalized, affirmations become a powerful tool for reinforcing positive beliefs and manifesting desires, ultimately resulting in positive actions and outcomes.

However, what most people don't tell you is that there is more to affirmations and manifesting than mere recitations or repetition of words. Of course, you have to "say it to see it" but if you do not strongly believe in your declarations and take adequate steps then you are bound to experience frustrations in your manifestation journey. Belief plays a key role in actualizing your affirmations.

For Black women in particular, affirmations have played a crucial role in promoting self-love, confidence, and self-esteem. In a world that often puts Black women at the intersection of multiple forms of societal marginalization, affirmations provide a space for us to affirm our beauty, worthiness, and abilities. They allow us to reclaim our strength and power in a society that has historically gaslit and undermined us.

Affirmations have been used as a tool of healing and resilience, passed down from generation to generation through oral tradition. For Black women, in particular, affirmations have become a form of self-care and a means to combat the daily oppression and microaggressions we face in our society.

Growing up, I remember my grandmother always telling me, "I am somebody." It wasn't until I got older that I realized that this was an affirmation that she used to instill confidence and self-worth in me. The affirmation of "I am enough" has become a mantra for many Black women, reminding us that we don't have to conform to society's beauty standards and that our value is not defined by our physical features.

Still don't believe it? Perhaps you would like a more scientific perspective. So, let's dive into the science behind affirmations.

The Science Behind Affirmations And Their Impact On The Subconscious Mind

From a scientific standpoint, affirmations work by rewiring our brains. Our subconscious minds are like a sponge, absorbing every thought and experience that we encounter. Our thoughts shape our reality, and if we constantly allow negative thoughts and experiences to occupy our minds, it can hinder our progress and emotional well-being. Affirmations reprogram our subconscious mind, allowing us to focus on positive thoughts and experiences.

Our thoughts create neural pathways in our brains, and these pathways form the basis for our attitudes, beliefs, and behaviors. When we regularly repeat positive affirmations, we create new neural pathways that reprogram our brains to embrace positive beliefs and habits. By repetition, we strengthen these pathways, and over time, they become our default thinking patterns.

When we repeat affirmations to ourselves, our mind begins to believe them, and our actions align with our beliefs. For example, if we repeat the affirmation, "I am successful," you have to have that positive feeling that confirms your belief in the words you are saying. When this feeling is present, our mind will begin to believe that we're successful, and we'll naturally put in the effort(action) to ensure that statement rings true in our reality. Affirmations have also been proven to reduce stress and anxiety, improve self-esteem, and increase happiness.

The science behind affirmations shows that our thoughts shape our reality. Affirmations help to reprogram your subconscious mind to focus on positivity. Remember, the words we speak have the power to create our reality; choose them wisely.

The power of affirmations deserves recognition and continues to be a crucial tool in facilitating positive change in our lives. The use of affirmations is not just for "self-help" but is a tool that has been used by our ancestors to get through hardships and strive for success. By understanding the cultural significance of affirmations and the science behind their impact, we can unlock their potential and allow them to transform our lives and communities. You must know that our ancestors believed in their declaration and took practical steps in ensuring that those words were given life to become their reality. Harriet Tubman didn't just say "I am free. I am happy. I am a powerful force for my people " before becoming a pivotal force in the underground railroad freeing both herself and hundreds of other slaves. No doubt, she said that affirmation with conviction, believed it and took action to make it a reality. We have to work in harmony with our thoughts, the same way those spiritually inclined persons know they have to work in harmony with their prayers.

Practical Tips For Crafting Effective And Empowering Affirmations

Affirmations can be tremendously powerful, yet many people are not sure how exactly to use them or might underestimate their true potential. They can be extremely effective in creating a more positive mindset and building self-confidence.

Let's delve into practical tips for crafting effective and empowering affirmations, share some inspiring affirmations that can help you build self-confidence, and discuss the power of positive self-talk in overcoming systemic challenges.

How To Craft Effective And Empowering Affirmations

The key to crafting effective affirmations is to make sure they resonate with you. You want to create affirmations that feel natural and authentic, so they can be easily integrated into your life.

Here are some practical tips for crafting empowering affirmations:

1. **Be specific:** Affirmations should be specific and meaningful to you. If you're really struggling with a particular issue, it's important to craft an affirmation that speaks directly to that issue. For instance, instead of just saying "I am successful," you might say "I am successful in my career and proud of my accomplishments."

2. **Use positive language:** Use positive language in your affirmations to create a more uplifting and empowering message. Instead of saying "I am not a failure," try saying "I am successful in all aspects of my life."

3. **Visualize:** Visualize your affirmations and imagine yourself embodying the message. This can help you connect more deeply with the affirmation and make it more powerful. This is also what makes vision boards so powerful.

4. **Don't compare yourself to others**: Avoid comparing yourself to others when crafting affirmations. Instead, focus on your own unique strengths and abilities. Your affirmations should reflect your journey and goals.

5. **Use the present tense:** Write affirmations in the present tense as if you have already achieved what you desire. This can help you believe in the affirmation and inspire you to take action.

6. **Make it realistic:** While it's important to aim high, make sure your affirmations are realistic. If you set a goal that seems impossible, it can be discouraging and counterproductive.

7. **Repeat regularly:** Consistency is key. Repeat your affirmations regularly, whether it's daily or multiple times a day. This can help reinforce the message and make it more natural to believe.

8. **Add emotion:** Adding emotion to your affirmations can make them more powerful. Imagine how you would feel when you achieve your desired outcome and infuse that emotion into your affirmation.

9. **Keep it short and simple:** Affirmations do not need to be long and complicated. Keep them short and simple to make them easy to remember and repeat throughout the day.

10. **Address Your Inner Critic:** Many times our inner critic holds us back from fulfilling our potential. That voice in our heads tells us that we can't do something or that we're not good enough. Crafting personalized affirmations that address your inner critic can be transformative. For example, "I am worthy of love and respect, no matter what my inner critic says." or "I am capable of making mistakes and learning from them." These affirmations

will help you silence the negative self-talk and make space for the positive mindset that you need to take action in order to grow.

Using the tips above you can make your own personalized affirmation list that caters to your life and experience.

However, if you are looking for some examples to work with here are some affirmations specifically tailored for Black women that can help build self-confidence and overcome adversity:

- I love and accept myself just the way I am.
- My Blackness is something to be proud of and celebrate.
- I am resilient in the face of adversity.
- I am powerful and capable of achieving anything I set my mind to.
- My beauty radiates from the inside out.

The Power of Positive Self-Talk

Positive self-talk is an essential part of building self-confidence and overcoming systemic challenges. It is a powerful tool that can help us cultivate a more positive attitude. When we use affirmations effectively and incorporate positive self-talk into our lives, we can become more resilient and empowered, better equipped to overcome even the most challenging obstacles.

When we speak to ourselves in a positive and affirming way, we can overcome negative self-talk and build a more optimistic outlook on life.

AFFIRMATION REVELATION

Positive self-talk involves consciously replacing negative thoughts and beliefs with positive ones. It means speaking to ourselves with compassion and encouragement instead of criticism and judgment. By changing the way we talk to ourselves, we can change the way we feel about ourselves and the world around us.

Research has shown that positive self-talk can have a significant impact on mental health and well-being. It can help reduce stress and anxiety, enhance resilience, and improve overall mood and self-esteem. Positive self-talk can also have a positive effect on physical health, such as decreasing inflammation and improving heart health.

Here are a few ways to incorporate positive self-talk into your daily life:

- **Affirmations:** Incorporate affirmations into your day-to-day life to create a more positive message for yourself. You might start by reciting an affirmation each morning before you start your day.

- **Focus on the positive:** Pay attention to the positive things in your life and try to cultivate a more positive attitude. This might mean focusing on your accomplishments instead of dwelling on failures.

- **Stop negative self-talk:** Recognize when negative self-talk creeps in and try to stop it in its tracks. Instead of saying "I can't do this," try saying "I am capable of doing this."

- **Focus on solutions, not problems:** When you encounter an obstacle, don't dwell on it. Instead, focus on finding a solution. This approach helps you to avoid negative self-talk, which can harm your confidence and self-esteem.

- **Practice self-compassion:** Be kind and understanding to yourself. Treat yourself like you would treat your best friend. When you make a mistake, don't beat yourself up. Instead, show yourself compassion and recognize that mistakes are learning opportunities.

- **Visualize success:** When you're facing a challenge, visualize yourself succeeding. Imagine the steps you need to take and how you'll feel when you overcome the challenge. This helps you to maintain a positive attitude and stay focused on your goals.

Being a Black woman can be a tough experience depending on where you live. In a world that often undervalues us and creates obstacles at every turn, it's important to remember that we are strong, resilient, and capable of achieving anything we set our minds to. As Black women, we have unique experiences and aspirations that deserve to be acknowledged and celebrated.

So, let's dive into some affirmations that specifically address our experiences and aspirations.

- I am proud of my Blackness and all that it represents. My culture and heritage are a source of strength and inspiration for me.

- Although people may try to tear me down, I will remain confident in myself and my abilities. I am worthy of success, love, and respect.

- My voice is important and deserves to be heard. I will not be silenced or marginalized by anyone, no matter how powerful they may seem.

AFFIRMATION REVELATION

- I am capable of achieving my dreams, no matter how big or audacious they may seem. I will not shy away from my goals but will work hard every day to make them a reality.

- As a black woman, I have faced many challenges, but I have also overcome them. This resilience has made me stronger and more determined to succeed.

- I am deserving of love and healthy relationships. I will not settle for less than I deserve and will wait for the right person to come into my life.

- Although it may be challenging, I will take the time to care for myself both physically and mentally. Self-care is an essential part of my well-being, and I will prioritize it.

- I will work to uplift and empower other black women. We are all in this together, and by supporting each other, we can create positive change in our communities.

- I am not defined by the stereotypes that society may try to pin on me. I am a complex and multifaceted individual with a unique personality, talents, and passions.

- Finally, I am proud of who I am and what I represent. As a Black woman, I am a trailblazer, a leader, and a force to be reckoned with. I will continue to push forward and make a positive impact on the world.

These affirmations are a starting point to remind you of your worth, inspire you to keep going, and motivate you to achieve your goals. Remember to take things one step at a time and celebrate every accomplishment, no matter how small. You are capable of greatness.

A Guide To Crafting Personalized Affirmations

Affirmations serve as reminders of your strengths and capabilities and can help you reframe your thoughts in a more positive light. By incorporating affirmations into your daily routine, you can change your mindset and boost your mood.

One of the most effective ways to use affirmations is by writing them down. Take some time to reflect on your strengths, values, and aspirations. What are your goals and what do you want to achieve? Use this introspection to create personalized affirmation statements that resonate with you. Write them down in a journal or on sticky notes, and place them in areas where you will see them regularly throughout the day.

For example, if your goal is to improve your confidence, your affirmation could be "I am confident and capable." Whenever you start to doubt yourself, repeat this phrase to yourself and remind yourself of your inner strength.

It's important to craft affirmations that are specific and meaningful to you. Instead of generic statements like "I am strong," think about what specifically makes you strong. Maybe it's your resilience in the face of challenges or your ability to remain calm under pressure. Crafting affirmations that focus on specific qualities you possess will make them more powerful and impactful in boosting your mindset.

Another helpful tip when crafting personalized affirmations is to use language that feels natural to you. It's okay to experiment with different phrasing until you find something that resonates with you. You might find that using present-tense statements like "I am" or "I have" are more effective, or perhaps using more action-oriented language like "I am taking steps towards" feels more meaningful.

Remember that affirmations are not just about saying positive things to yourself; they need to be supported by **action.** Use your affirmations as inspiration to take concrete steps toward your goals and aspirations. For example, if one of your affirmations is "*I am capable of achieving my dreams,*" use that motivation to create a plan to achieve those dreams and take actionable steps towards them every day.

Overall, crafting personalized affirmations can be a powerful tool in changing your mindset and achieving your goals. Take time to reflect on what matters to you, use specific language that resonates with you, and support your affirmations with action to truly harness your power.

Reflecting on the Impact of Affirmations

As you start using affirmations, keep track of the impact they have on your mindset and mood. Set aside time in your day to journal and reflect on your experiences with affirmations. How did repeating your affirmations make you feel? Did you notice any changes in your thoughts or emotions? Did you find it easier to push through challenging moments?

Soulful Scribbles:

Here are some journaling prompts to get you started:

How have my affirmations helped me reframe my thoughts?

....
....
....
....
....
....
....
....

What impact have my affirmations had on my confidence and self-esteem?

....
....
....
....
....
....
....

AFFIRMATION REVELATION

How have my affirmations helped me cope with stress and anxiety?

....

....

....

....

....

....

....

....

Reflecting on the impact of affirmations can also help you to refine your practice. For example, if you notice that you're not seeing the results you want, you may want to adjust the wording of your affirmations or try a different approach. Or, if you find that affirmations are working well for you, you may want to experiment with new affirmations that build on your existing practice.

Reflecting on the impact of affirmations can help you better understand how this practice is affecting your life. Keeping track of your experiences with affirmations can be a helpful way to measure your progress, notice patterns, and identify areas where you need to focus your efforts.

ACTIVITY: Design Affirmation Cards or Booklet You Can Use Daily

For those who love arts and crafts and creative expression, activities like designing affirmation cards or a mini affirmation booklet can be helpful. Choose some of your favorite affirmations and design visually appealing graphics that you can use for daily inspiration. You can compile them into a small booklet or keep them as separate cards. The key is to create something that motivates and uplifts you.

By crafting personalized affirmations, reflecting on their impact, and using them regularly, you can unlock their full potential. So, take some time to reflect on your strengths and goals, and start incorporating affirmations into your daily life. You'll be amazed at the positive changes you'll see in your thoughts and emotions.

Changing your thoughts is the first step to slaying the illusion society continuously casts upon us. We need to give ourselves permission to change the narrative. Meet me in the next chapter where we will discuss next steps on how to break free and unapologetically shine our brilliant light on the world.

> "You are the one that possesses the keys to your being. You carry the passport to your own happiness."

— DIANE VON FURSTENBERG

Chapter 3

Slaying The Illusion:
Liberating Black Women From Shallow Tactics With Unapologetic Brilliance

As Black women, we are often expected to fit into certain molds that have been created for us by society. We're supposed to act a certain way, dress a certain way, talk a certain way, and be a certain type of woman. But you know what? I'm tired of it. I'm tired of being told how to live my life and how to be successful.

So, in this chapter, we're going to slay the illusion that has been placed upon us and liberate ourselves from the shallow tactics that society has forced upon us.

This is not just another chapter in a book. It's a call to action for all Black women who are tired of playing by societal rules that were never even designed to accommodate us.

We're going to be unapologetically brilliant!

As a Black woman myself, I understand firsthand how disheartening it can be to constantly encounter and navigate through the systemic barriers and societal expectations that limit our potential. Despite the progress our society has made toward gender equality, Black women still experience a great deal of adversity from both within and outside of our communities. These challenges include discrimination, misogyny, and stereotyping.

One of the most prevalent issues plaguing us as Black women is the tendency to succumb to shallow tactics to fit societal standards and expectations. To liberate ourselves from these shallow tactics, we must learn how to embrace our unapologetic brilliance, reject societal barriers, and reclaim our power. A clear example is Katherine Johnson who defied all odds not just as a woman but a Black woman to help NASA put a man on the moon through her calculations of orbital mechanics. She did this at the time racial segregation was at its all time high and the opportunities available to women were very limited so it can be said that she broke two glass ceilings with her exploit at NASA.

How can you do this? By slaying the illusion that society has been built for Black women.

Slaying the Illusion

Slaying the illusion requires that we understand the societal constructs that have created the shallow tactics that we fall victim to. Historically, our identities as Black women have been restricted to only a few stereotypical roles such as being a mammy or the angry Black woman. We are often stereotyped as being aggressive, loud, and unprofessional. Unfortunately, these stereotypes can affect how people perceive us in social situations. It's important to recognize that these stereotypes are not a reflection of who we are, and we shouldn't limit ourselves to fit them.

We are expected to carry the weight of our race and gender on our shoulders, while still maintaining a level of beauty and grace that is often unattainable. Hence, we are stuck in this toxic cycle where we constantly feel pressure to fit into the mold that has been created for us. As opposed to embracing our individuality and brilliance. Well, it is time to break free.

How can you slay these illusions? You can do so by taking control of your reality. You must recognize your innate, authentic power. You are capable of manifesting anything you desire. It is therefore essential that you focus on building self-belief and self-love. How can you do this? By intentional manifestations, not the superficial stuff that seems to be getting all the rave now. This would allow you to truly see yourself for who you are and not the illusions society projects.

Embracing Authenticity: A Deeper Path to Manifestation for Black Women

In a world that often tries to define who we should be, it can be a radical act for Black women to embrace their authenticity. Society's expectations, media portrayals, and personal experiences can often lead Black women to conform to certain roles and behaviors. However, embracing authenticity is not only a powerful act of self-love, but it also opens doors to a deeper path of manifestation.

Authenticity is not merely about being true to oneself, but also about reclaiming one's identity and honoring the rich history and culture that

Black women bring to the table. It's about shedding the armor we've built to protect ourselves from a world that has not always valued us, and stepping into our power unapologetically.

For Black women, embracing authenticity can seem like a daunting task. We often find ourselves navigating through stereotypes and harmful narratives that have shaped our experiences. Society tells us to be strong, but not too assertive. To be ambitious, but not too ambitious. To be beautiful, but not in a way that challenges Eurocentric standards. The pressure to conform can be overwhelming, but it is within the realm of our authenticity that true manifestation lies.

While we've all heard about manifesting by simply visualizing our desires, it's important to acknowledge the limitations of these superficial techniques. Merely repeating affirmations or creating vision boards can often overlook the complex realities we face as Black women. We have our own unique set of challenges, deeply rooted in historical and societal contexts. So, it's time we break free from the mold and explore practical tools that truly resonate with our experiences.

When we embrace our authenticity, we release the limiting beliefs and societal expectations that have held us back. We begin to tap into our unique gifts and talents that have been waiting to be expressed. We let go of the need to conform, instead embracing our natural rhythm, style, and voice. This authenticity becomes a beacon, attracting opportunities and relationships that align with our true selves.

Authenticity also allows us to reclaim our narrative. It gives us the power to define ourselves, rather than allowing others to define us. By embracing our authenticity, we challenge the stereotypes and narratives that have overshadowed our brilliance. We become the authors of our own stories, paving the way for future generations of Black women to shine authentically.

Furthermore, embracing authenticity creates a ripple effect of empowerment and liberation. When we embrace who we truly are, we inspire others to do the same. We become role models for those who have been told their authenticity is a liability rather than an asset. Our journey becomes a testament to the power of embracing all aspects of ourselves, even the parts that society may deem undesirable.

It is essential to note that embracing authenticity does not mean disregarding or erasing the challenges Black women face. Rather, it is about acknowledging and honoring those challenges while still embracing our authentic selves. It is about finding strength in our vulnerabilities and using them as catalysts for growth and transformation.

We have a unique perspective and voice that deserves to be heard and celebrated. Embracing authenticity allows us to manifest a life that honors our true selves and allows us to create meaningful change in our communities. It is a path that may be challenging at times, but one that is filled with immense beauty, power, and endless possibilities.

Pitfalls Of Superficial Manifestation Techniques

Most manifestation techniques follow similar principles - visualize, believe, and receive. However, some individuals focus solely on the receiving part, neglecting the importance of belief. This often results in superficial manifestation techniques that prioritize quick results over long-term goals. Black women are often pressured to conform to these shallow techniques that prioritize external validation, leading to a never-ending cycle of self-doubt and disappointment. It's important to recognize that manifestation is a journey, not a quick fix. Focusing solely on external validation will not bring long-term happiness. So how can you ensure that you are not on the superficial manifestation train?

Practical Techniques For Black Queens

Now, let's talk practicality! Here are a few techniques tailored to resonate with our unique experiences as Black queens:

1. **Authentic Self-Expression:** Permit yourself to authentically express who you are. Make space for your voice, creativity, and passions. Whether it's journaling, painting, or dancing, find a form of self-expression that resonates with you and helps you manifest from a place of truth.

2. **Embrace Ancestral Wisdom:** Connect with the incredible strength and resilience of your ancestors. Learn about their struggles, wisdom, and traditions. Speak affirmations in your native language to tap into this powerful source of manifestation energy.

3. **Supportive Sisterhood**: Surround yourself with a diverse network of fellow Black women who support your dreams and uplift your aspirations. Nurture friendships where you can share experiences, ideas, and insights. By creating a community of like-minded souls, you can amplify your manifestation journey.

4. **Mindful Affirmations:** Tailor affirmations to your unique experiences as a Black woman. Focus on affirmations that speak directly to your power, beauty, resilience, and cultural heritage. The more specific and personal, the stronger the manifestation energy.

Liberating Black Women With Unapologetic Brilliance

The most effective way to liberate ourselves is to embrace our unapologetic brilliance. Unapologetic brilliance involves accepting our unique experiences and identities as Black women, understanding our values, and using our voices to advocate for ourselves and others. We must refuse to be silenced by societal pressures and expectations.

We can start by dismantling the systemic barriers that limit our opportunities and hinder our progress. This entails seeking out opportunities for education, professional advancement, and financial independence. As we do this, we must also advocate for better policies and practices that promote equal opportunities for Black women and other marginalized groups.

We also need to actively challenge and reject the shallow tactics that society expects us to adopt. This means refusing to conform to societal beauty standards, rejecting stereotypes, and setting our own standards for success.

Deepening Your Connection To Your Subconscious

You can cultivate transformative shifts in confidence and self-worth by applying mindful meditation techniques. By silencing external noise and connecting with your inner self, you can summon the strength to pursue your passions, overcome obstacles and achieve remarkable success. Cultivating self-worth and confidence is vital in the manifestation process. To enhance these qualities, Black women can address self-doubt, fear, and limiting beliefs head-on, harnessing the full potential of their subconscious minds to manifest their dreams. Here are a few we can examine further:

Saran Kaba Jones. Saran Kaba Jones is another inspirational figure. Growing up in Liberia during a civil war, Saran's family fled to the United States when she was just 10 years old. Despite facing significant challenges with the civil war in her home country, settling in the US with an immigrant family, Saran remained focused and determined to break free and succeed and that she did. She also stayed true to her background and she used what she faced in a war-torn country to launch a non-profit organization called FACE Africa. Through her organization, Saran has brought clean water and sanitation to communities throughout sub-Saharan Africa, transforming countless lives in the process.

Ava DuVernay is a talented filmmaker whose work has made a significant impact on Hollywood. Despite facing many barriers in the industry, Ava has always remained true to her vision and values, creating films that challenge the status quo and promote social justice. Her film "Selma" tells the story of the civil rights movement in the 1960s, while her series "Queen Sugar" highlights the experiences of Black families in the American South where she highlights blacks had to undergo just to get by in a heavily racially segregated society.

As a passionate and purposeful Black woman, I, myself also understood that I had to put in the work to make a mark. I navigated the hustle of New York to build a career as a public school teacher, educational consultant, author and business coach. Life wasn't always easy for me. On the outside it appeared I had the perfect family, living in a middle class household with both parents and being raised in a religious household. But, behind closed walls my father was an abusive alcoholic. The trauma from living in that household definitely impacted me negatively especially in my teenage years. But, I vowed never to let myself fall and fail. I have a family of my own that deserves love and compassion and I strive to give them that daily. To this day, my vow still stands to continuously define what success looks like for me, and consistently put in the work to make it a reality.

These are just a few examples of Black women who have broken free from superficial techniques and achieved success by remaining true to themselves and their values working tirelessly to empower others and make a real difference in the world. These stories are an inspiration to us all, reminding us that with dedication and hard work, we too can achieve greatness and make a lasting impact. Who do you admire that has also embraced practical techniques for success?

Here are some exercises you can do to help you break free from superficial techniques and assist in practical strategies for success.

Exercise 1: Journaling for Self-Exploration

One powerful exercise to deepen your connection with your subconscious mind is regular journaling. By allowing your thoughts and emotions to flow freely onto paper, you will gain valuable insights into your deepest desires, fears, and limiting beliefs.

Begin by setting aside time each day to write without judgment or filter. Explore your dreams, ambitions, and obstacles, allowing your subconscious mind to reveal hidden patterns and opportunities for growth. Many Black women have found solace and clarity through journaling, leading to transformative changes in their lives.

Exercise 2: Visualization for Manifestation

Visualization is a potent tool to manifest your desires and deepen your connection with your subconscious mind. Take a few moments each day to visualize yourself already living your dream life. Immerse yourself in the emotions and sensations of achieving your goals.

Real-life examples of Black women who have harnessed the power of visualization are abundant. From entrepreneurs breaking barriers to artists shattering expectations, these women have used visualization to overcome obstacles and achieve lasting success. Read and study their stories to serve as powerful inspirations for anyone seeking to leverage their subconscious mind.

Exercise 3: Mindful Meditation and Mindfulness-Based Practices

Mindful meditation is instrumental in enhancing the connection with your subconscious mind. By focusing on the present moment, you create space for self-reflection and heightened self-awareness. Incorporate mindfulness practices into your daily routine to cultivate a deeper understanding of yourself, your thoughts, and your emotions. We'll delve deeper into strategies to enhance self-worth and confidence in a later chapter.

Empowering Affirmations for Inner Healing

Inner healing is a powerful process that allows you to address past traumas and emotional wounds, freeing your subconscious mind from their chains. Utilizing empowering affirmations aimed at self-worth and inner healing can facilitate this transformative journey.

By incorporating affirmations such as "I am worthy of love and success," "I release all negative energy that no longer serves me," and "I am deserving of abundance and joy," you can reprogram your subconscious mind, deepening your connection with yourself and accelerating your personal growth.

Here are some examples that you can use:

- I am deserving of love and respect.
- I trust in my own abilities and intuition.
- I release any negative beliefs about myself that no longer serve me.
- I am enough just as I am.
- I am worthy of happiness and success.
- I choose to focus on my strengths and accomplishments.
- I am capable of creating positive change in my life.
- I embrace my unique qualities and let my authentic self shine.
- I let go of past hurts and forgive myself and others.

- I am worthy of love and belonging.
- I am grateful for my experiences and learn from them.
- I am kind and compassionate to myself and others.
- I am confident in who I am and what I bring to the world.
- I trust the journey of my life and embrace the lessons it brings.
- I honor my emotions and give myself permission to feel and heal.

Reflect and Empower: Breaking Free from Superficial Techniques

We live in a world where quick fixes and superficial techniques dominate our daily lives. We are bombarded with advertisements promising instant success, happiness, and fulfillment. However, these shallow methods often leave us feeling empty, unsatisfied, and yearning for something more meaningful.

It's time to break free from superficial techniques and tap into our inner power to manifest our dreams authentically. Let us explore a list of common superficial techniques, engage in a belief restructuring exercise, and delve into alternative methods for deepening our manifestation practice.

Common Superficial Techniques:

1. Affirmations: While repeating positive affirmations can be a useful tool for creating a positive mindset, their effectiveness diminishes when they lack genuine belief and alignment with our core values and desires. Take a moment to reflect on the effectiveness of affirmations in your life. Are they helping you create real change, or are they merely empty words?

2. **Visualization:** Visualization can be a powerful tool for manifestation, but it becomes superficial when it lacks depth and emotional connection. Reflect on your visualization practice. Are you engaging all your senses in these visualizations? Do they evoke strong emotions and truly ignite your passion and drive?

3. **Gratitude Journaling:** Gratitude journaling has gained popularity in recent years and is undoubtedly beneficial for shifting our focus to the positive aspects of our lives. However, it can become superficial when we only express gratitude for the surface-level benefits without truly connecting to the underlying feelings of appreciation and abundance. Take a moment to examine your gratitude practice. Are you genuinely feeling the emotions of gratitude or merely going through the motions? What are you truly thankful for? How can you display gratitude on a deeper level daily?

ACTIVITY: Identifying and challenging limiting beliefs through a belief restructuring exercise

Superficial techniques often fail to address the root cause of our limitations - our limiting beliefs. By identifying and challenging these beliefs, we can pave the way for genuine transformation and manifestation. So here is a fun exercise.

Take a blank sheet of paper and write down one limiting belief that has held you back from manifesting your desires. Reflect on this belief and ask yourself, "Is this belief true? What evidence do I have to support it? What evidence contradicts it?"

Now, reframe this belief by turning it into a positive, empowering statement below. For example, if your limiting belief is "I am not capable of achieving success," rewrite it as "I have the skills, knowledge, and determination to achieve incredible success."

Finally, write down three actions you can take right now to challenge this limiting belief and move towards your desired outcome.

1. ....

2. ....

3. ....

Soulful Scribbles

Journal Writing prompts to explore alternative methods for deepening the manifestation practice:

Connection with Self: How can I deepen my connection with myself to align my desires and beliefs with who I truly am?

....
....
....
....
....
....
....

Intention Setting: How can I enhance my intention-setting process to ensure that I am setting clear, authentic, and aligned intentions?

....
....
....
....
....
....
....

Emotional Alchemy: How can I tap into my emotions and use them as a guiding force in my manifestation practice?

....

....

....

....

....

....

....

Inner Work: How can I integrate inner work practices such as shadow work, self-reflection, and forgiveness to uncover and release subconscious blocks?

....

....

....

....

....

....

....

Action and Alignment: How can I take inspired and aligned action towards my desires, trusting that the universe will meet me halfway?

....

....

....

....

....

....

....

....

Remember, the true magic lies in your ability to connect with yourself and trust in the process of manifestation.

"Change your thoughts, change your ways."

—NORMAN VINCENT PEALE

Chapter 4

Aligning with Your True Desires:
The Blueprint for Rewriting Your Subconscious for Lasting Success

Where are you right now in your life? Really think about it, are you where *you* want to be in life? Or, are you where societal narratives placed you?

It is easy for women to relegate themselves and even push their true desires aside for the good of their spouses, children, families, friends, and colleagues. Over time, this attitude of "self last" becomes detrimental and damaging to personal and professional growth.

This chapter holds a profound and in-depth meaning for many women who faced challenges and systemic barriers limiting them from moving ahead throughout history. Rewriting your subconscious is the first step to aligning your true desires for lasting success. It involves a compelling process of introspection, self-discovery, and intentionality – you have to be in a place of awareness that ensures you know what you are doing at every point and is a part of it.

For women, this means stepping away from societal norms that limit and stagnate them and replacing them with empowering truth or affirmation that dismantles years of inferiority complex, doubt, and unworthiness rooted in our subconscious via slavery, racism, and gender inequality. It means letting go of all the shackles into a position of authentic power that unleashes your true potential.

However, by rewriting the subconscious, women can recognize these rooted peculiar challenges and cultivate a mindset of resilience, success, abundance, intelligence, talent, self-worth, and self-belief. Furthermore, this chapter is crafted to help you recognize these barriers and offer practical strategies to overcome them.

The role of the subconscious mind in the manifestation

Whether you like it or not, the sub-subconscious mind plays a pivotal role in your manifestation, by influencing your thoughts, beliefs, and behaviors. It stores deeply ingrained beliefs and conditioning that shape our reality and immensely affect our decisions now or in the future.

Chances are you are heading for failure or will not attract the desired outcomes if you fail to align your subconscious mind with positive affirmations, visualization, empowering beliefs, and conditions that project your manifestation.

As discussed earlier, for Black women, the subconscious mind is influenced by several external factors that are then internalized as normal such as cultural conditioning, internalized oppression, and societal stereotypes. Overcoming these influences and cultivating a strong sense of empowerment through the subconscious mind is crucial for proper manifestation rather than leaving things to chance.

Here's how the subconscious mind affects manifestation specifically for Black women:

Cultural conditioning includes norms, values, and beliefs instilled within a particular culture and can be traced to ancestral and generational traumas or traditions within a family. Black women may have been conditioned to believe certain limitations or stereotypes about their capabilities, beauty standards, or opportunities. For example, women are to be submissive and tend to their men, women should put the needs of the family first and their needs last, or women should not be vocal and outspoken and so many more.

These cultural beliefs are deep wounds that have secluded women, black women especially and pushed them into silence while suffering abuses of various kinds. The subconscious mind absorbs these societal narratives reinforcing them, thereby affecting their manifestation efforts.

Healing ancestral and generational traumas is of utmost importance for Black women's empowerment as these traumas challenge the narratives that seek to diminish their worth and reclaim their identities and voices. By healing, you can reclaim their power, stand tall in your truth, and contribute to dismantling systemic barriers, and breaking down systematic abuses, deep wounds, and pains passed down from one generation to the next.

There is no denying that traumas have a profound impact on the psychological, emotional, and physical well-being of Black women today. However, acknowledging this, empowers black women to transcend limiting beliefs, negative self-perceptions, and internalized racism that hinder progress.

Think about how this impacts you directly. It also allows you to create their own narrative in healthier environments for future generations, promoting resilience and empowerment. You have the power to change the narrative, become a role model, and inspire others to embark on their own healing journeys.

Overcoming Internalized Oppression

Think about how many subconscious messages you internalize everyday about who you are and who society projects you should be. Think about the reality shows that popularize Black women attacking one another by being dressed in some of the top designers, dining in some of the finest restaurants)with rich men), but screaming expletives and insults while throwing their overpriced drinks in the faces of one another. What message is being sent here during prime time tv? Or how about only seeing lighter skinned women be perceived as beautiful in movies, kid shows, music videos and popular magazines? What about the microaggressions encountered at the workplace, where you feel constantly overlooked and have to prepare twice as hard and earn more letters to place behind your name on an email signature, just so you can be *considered* for a promotion?

When I taught English at a high school in the inner city, I was constantly second guessed by my colleagues and even those with higher authority. When I visited organizations for professional development, I still was asked to show I.D. and state where I taught, while my Caucasian colleagues simply signed their attendance and waltzed into rooms. I had to check myself and evaluate not only how I perceived my colleagues, but how I perceived myself as well.

These oppressive internalizations are not only detrimental to self-love, self-growth, confidence and esteem but also how you perceive other women of color as well.

The solution is not as easy as a hot knife passing through butter, but it is achievable.

- **Learn to identify internalized oppression** and its impact through self awareness and education. This enables you to question the statuesque. When you begin to feel sad, angry or even critical of yourself or another, ask yourself "why" to get to the root of the issue. Then begin meditating, journaling or talking to a professional about strategies as to how to overcome it.

- **Do not think you are not affected by oppression and microaggressions** of the modern world we live in; hence conduct a thorough assessment of your self-worth, examining your beliefs and attitudes. Be kind to yourself and speak kindly to yourself. Listen to how you speak or think about yourself, is it usually positive or negative? Ensure you are being your own best friend.

- **Find a community of Black women** to hasten the healing and enable you to channel the power of internalized oppression through dialogues, support, and sharing of their personal experiences. Support is vital.

- **Watch what you ingest from the medi**a about societal narratives by questioning platforms that reinforce oppressive beliefs and degrade Black women. Social media and the news are breeding grounds for displaying these passive oppressive beliefs, be mindful as to how much time you are spending on these platforms and limit them.

- **Find mentors and participate actively** in actions that promote social justice, inclusion, guidance, equality, healing, and self-care that will help others and other women of color in your community.

Remember that overcoming internalized oppression is an ongoing process. Be patient and kind to yourself as you navigate this journey. However, healing allows you to celebrate your progress and acknowledge the strength and resilience it takes to challenge and dismantle internalized oppression.

Emotional Energy and Vibrational Alignment

Back in the 50s or 60s, some radios used large knobs to enable users to search the frequency to get to their desired audio program. These stations were only heard clearly and audibly when you were aligned properly on the channel you desired. Likewise, your journey to success, love, financial freedom, etc will only be clear if your desires are aligned.

So, the question is:

- What are you aligned with today?
- What frequency are you attuned to?
- What energy source are you drawing your power from?

The subconscious mind is closely connected to emotions and energy. Emotions serve as a powerful magnet for manifestation, and the subconscious mind processes and responds to emotional states. Black women must align their subconscious minds to positive emotions such as gratitude, joy, love, freedom, capacity, and self-belief, as these high-vibrational states attract their desired experience. Being mindful of your emotional energy and consciously directing it towards positive manifestations can greatly enhance your results.

By actively reshaping and reprogramming your subconscious beliefs, you can align yourself with empowering narratives that support your desires and goals.

Reprogram your subconscious to improve your manifestation. While emotional energy and vibrational alignment are effective pathways to raise your vibrational frequency, here is a technique that can help: - manifest your desires and visualize your goals through a vision board.

There is a Buddhist quote I love and it embodies the significance of visualization and using vision boards to attract your desires.

> " What you think, you become. What you feel, you attract. What you imagine you create."

Simple, yet powerful; the truth is, you cannot be what you cannot envision. If you cannot see it, you cannot feel, think or imagine it.

What is a vision board?

It is a board that consists of a snippet of your desires, affirmations or positive thoughts that represent where you are, want to be and how to get there. It is like a road map or GPS system that keeps you aligned on your personal journey.

Vision boards can help you by:

ALIGNING WITH YOUR TRUE DESIRES

- Continuously reminding you of your purpose and goal
- Assisting in defining the clarity of your purpose
- Helping you stay within the intent of your purpose
- Building the focus and determination needed to succeed
- Helping you visualize how close/far away you are along your journey

Are you new to vision boards and their power to birth your manifestations? I have provided quick access to vision board clip art books especially designed for Black women and moms to help you jumpstart the process no matter where you are on your journey. Just scan the QR codes and you will be one step closer to your vision board success.

Here is a recap on why vision boards are amazing;

Desires are the goals, ambitions, and aspirations that individuals hold on to or want to see done in their life. They serve as guiding lights, direction, and motivation for the desired result. Identifying and understanding your desires is crucial because they act as a compass, guiding actions toward meaningful outcomes. When desires align with beliefs and actions, more black women will enjoy a sense of satisfaction and purpose.

- **Beliefs** are the ingrained convictions, values, and perspectives that influence how people perceive themselves, others, and the world around them. Individuals experience a stronger sense of authenticity when beliefs align with desires. For example, if you desire to contribute to building a community of strong Black girls, yet believe that these girls are all doomed for failure based on where they live or lack of education then your desires will conflict as they do not match. Aligning desires with empowering and positive beliefs fosters clarity, confidence, and a greater sense of personal integrity.

- **Actions** are the tangible steps to manifest desires and beliefs in the physical world. It is the bridge between intentions and outcomes. Aligning actions with desires and beliefs ensures that individuals actively work towards their goals and values. Consistent and intentional action-taking is essential for personal growth and progress. Without alignment, individuals may experience a sense of stagnation, frustration, or self-sabotage as their actions contradict their true desires and beliefs.

Now, go back to that list you created of your desires and motivations. Do they align? If not, figure out what needs to be done to keep them in alignment so that your actions are not contradictory and doomed for failure

The importance of alignment between desires, beliefs, and actions can be summarized through the following key points:

- **Authenticity and Integrity**: When desires, beliefs, and actions align, individuals experience a greater sense of authenticity and integrity. They live by their unique values, fostering a stronger sense of self and building trust within themselves and others.

- **Focus and Clarity:** Alignment provides a clear vision of what one wants to achieve and how to get there. It eliminates confusion, indecisiveness, and distractions, enabling individuals to prioritize actions directly linked to their desires and beliefs.

- **Motivation and Resilience:** When desires are aligned with beliefs and actions, individuals become highly motivated, determined, and resilient. They have a compelling reason to pursue their goals and are more likely to overcome obstacles and setbacks along the way.

- **Well-being and Satisfaction**: Living in alignment promotes a feeling of fulfillment and well-being. When individuals consistently act by their desires and beliefs, they experience a deep sense of satisfaction and contentment, knowing they are living a life true to themselves.

- **Impact and Success:** Alignment enhances the effectiveness and impact of your actions. By aligning desires and beliefs with actions, individuals optimize their efforts, increase productivity, and achieve success in life.

- **Reflect and Repower:** A simple exercise to help you with alignment and subconscious reprogramming.

- **Visualize your day:** Every morning before you get out of bed, visualize the perfect day. Visualize what is in it, how it will work, and what results you expect for the day.

- **Create an affirmation list:** Nothing good comes easy, and affirmations are certainly not a get-there-quick scheme. It is a continuous and consistent action that gradually aligns your desires by reprogramming your subconscious mind. For example, if wealth and riches are a desire, daily repeating - *"I am a wealth magnet, and wealth comes to me effortlessly"* - will be the *starting point* in using your internal compass to point you in the right direction.

Here are 3 strategies you can use to assist you in gaining clarity and alignment:

Emotional Freedom Technique

Emotional Freedom Technique (EFT) is a therapeutic method that combines acupressure with psychology. The process works by tapping on specific energy points on the body to release blockage and enable emotional balance. This technique helps to dislodge bad energy and emotions while verbalizing positive affirmations. Here are the steps below:

- **Identify the problem:** It could be a specific emotion, thought, or issue that invokes fear, anxiety, negative belief, past trauma, or any emotional disturbance.

- **Setup statement:** Create a setup statement that acknowledges the issue and affirms self-acceptance. For example, "Even though I have a fear of public speaking, I deeply and completely accept myself."

- **Tapping sequence:** While repeating your setup statement, tap on specific acupressure points on your body. Some are various points around the eye, collarbone, under the nose, under the arm and chin. You can tap gently with your fingertips or use a few fingers together. You can do this about 10 to 12 times depending on your schedule and the stage you are at mentally and physically and each should last a minimum of 2 minutes.

- **Reminder phrase:** After a few rounds of tapping, use a reminder phrase to summarize the issue. For example, "The fear of public speaking" or "The anxiety in my stomach." This stage is basically you summarizing what you are tapping about and making sure your focus is as clear as it should be.

- **Repeat and reassess:** Continue tapping and repeating the process while focusing on the issue. After you are done with a series of sessions you need to reassess the intensity of the emotion or thought. This process aims to reduce the power of emotion and create a sense of calm and balance.

Journaling

As mentioned in Chapter 1, journaling is a simple technique that monitors your daily progress about the good, the bad, and the ugly. Journaling your desires and intentions in a book or on your electronic device, helps you to describe what/how you are feeling in detail and explore the emotions associated with their fulfillment.

Journaling allows you to clarify your desires, uncover limiting beliefs, and create a stronger connection with your subconscious mind.

How to start journaling?

Get a book – a journal and a set of pens (different colors preferably, green for happy days, red for sad days, blue for hopeful days, the color choice is yours).

One each day write:

- A title (optional)
- Expectations for the day – even the minute details
- How you are feeling at the moment – adding any significant mentions
- What you are grateful for and why

- Your daily manifestation and positive affirmations that backs them up. For example, "I will fulfill all my tasks. I am strong and can do it.
- List three goals you achieved for the day/hope to achieve for the next day
- When you wake up, visualize how you want your day to be and evaluate how your day went before going to bed.

The time spent journaling depends on you – it can be as short as 5 minutes or as long as an hour. Remember, it is your "me-time," use it wisely.

Positive Self-talk and Personal Accountability

Pay attention to your internal dialogue and self-talk. Notice any negative or limiting beliefs that may contradict your desires. Replace them with positive and empowering thoughts. Speak to yourself as if you have already achieved your desires, reinforcing the belief that they are possible and within reach.

> *Stick with your routine - Consistency is the key to success, you will get tired but do not give up.*

Throughout history, some Black women have rewired their subconscious for lasting success. Today, we have black women everywhere, from politics to science, film, and more. Their pursuit, whether to narrow the wealth gap or fight for freedom, or demonstrate their strength and perseverance is glaring for the common good of society.

Some women that have broken the statuesque are:

- **Mary McLeod.** She was a slave who emphasized the significance of education to colored children and founded the Daytona Educational and Industrial Institute for Girls. Similar to the famous TV personality, Oprah.

- **Tarana Burke** is another significant woman of our era. If her name sounds unfamiliar, then the #MeToo movement is not. She is the founder of the movement and a powerful voice against sexual abuse and violence against women.

- **Mae Jemison** was the first woman admitted to the astronaut program and the first to fly in space. Read her story about overcoming adversity and self doubt as well.

- **Michelle Obama** is also still a household name today. While she is not the first woman of color in politics, she is the first black woman to serve as first lady of the USA. There are many more, but these women prove you can do anything you desire, if you believe in it and work toward it.

This chapter demonstrates to all black women that "align with their true desire" is not a mere statement but a transformational tool that shatters limitations and societal narratives about women that emphasize self-care, self-love, and the enjoyment of lasting success in all aspects of their lives.

Reflect and Empower: Rewiring Your Subconscious for Lasting Success

> **Visualization exercises** to engage the subconscious mind and reinforce desired beliefs.

As stated multiple times throughout the book, visualization exercises help rewrite the subconscious allowing you to envision and manifest your dreams and aspirations by harnessing the power of envisioning your end goal, positive affirmations, and intentional goal-setting. This process empowers you to overcome obstacles, tap into your innate creativity, and take inspired action toward your goals. Scan the QR code at the back of the book for the vision board clip art books to help you get started with visualization exercises.

- Create a personalized affirmation playlist or audio recording
- Check through your journal and list your personal or professional goals and aspirations for the week, month or year
- Identify areas of strength and weaknesses and where you need improvement
- If you have a hard time writing your own affirmations, Google ones that address your weaknesses
- Remember to keep your affirmations short, memorable, positive and present.
- Use music or sound to create a conducive atmosphere
- Record your affirmations on your phone or another device and listen to them daily

ACTIVITY: Develop a daily affirmation practice routine and track progress over time

- Set aside a specific time each day for your affirmation practice, such as in the morning or before bed.
- Keep your environment quiet
- Practice breathing techniques to calm your mind
- Replay your affirmation recording
- Go through your journal and read your daily write up aloud
- Assess your progress and write it down – score as follows:

1 **On Cloud Nine:** Feeling amazing and ready to conquer the world with my positive affirmations and journaling practice.

2 **Smooth Sailing:** My affirmations and journaling are going well, with occasional bumps in the road.

3 **Fair to Middling:** I'm making some progress, but there's room for improvement in my routine.

4 **Hitting Speed Bumps:** My affirmations and journaling practice needs a little more attention and effort to get back on track.

5 **Lost in the Fog:** Uh-oh, it seems like I've veered off course with my affirmations and journaling. Time to reevaluate and make some changes.

BEYOND AFFIRMATIONS

Ultimately, rewriting the subconscious for lasting success offers you a pathway to holistic personal growth, helps you to acknowledge your unique experiences, foster self-acceptance, and nurture self-love. As you continue, you will gradually begin to love yourself more and have enough to unleash to the world. In the next chapter we will delve deep into this and show you how to unleash the true power of self love.

"Love yourself fiercely, for within the depths of your being resides an unbreakable spirit that deserves all the tenderness, compassion, and adoration in the world."

- AUDRE LORDE

Chapter 5

Love Unleashed:
The Empowered Equation for Self-Worth, Self-Love, and Your Inner Sparkle

Welcome to the chapter that's going to teach you how to embrace the most powerful force in the universe: *love.* That's right, we're talking about Love Unleashed and how it can change your life for the better.

In a world where social media filters and curated profiles seem to overshadow authenticity. it's easy to fall into the trap of self-doubt and comparison. But there is a powerful force that unlocks the true sense of self-worth, self-love, and your inner sparkle and that's Love. Love without a doubt is the most profound and transformative emotion that influences how we see ourselves and here we will break down the power of self-love and provide practical insights on how you can harness it to set yourself free and shine your light unapologetically.

Self-worth is an essential component of our well-being and happiness. When we value ourselves, we experience a sense of purpose, confidence, and inner peace.

There is nothing more beautiful than a woman who radiates confidence, self-love, and genuine happiness. As Black women, we are often faced with cultural influences and societal stereotypes that can negatively impact our self-esteem. For far too long, Black women have been denied the privilege of feeling beautiful and worthy of love simply because of the color of our skin or the texture of our hair.

In all honesty, fostering a positive self-image can be a challenging journey given the societal stereotypes that surround us. From being told to alter our hair texture to fit into Eurocentric beauty standards to being labeled as "sassy" or "angry," there are various external factors that can impact our view of ourselves. However, it is important to remember that true self-worth and self-love come from within.

In this chapter, we will explore the intersection of self-worth, self-love, and confidence in the context of Black womanhood and how we can unleash love to ignite the sparkle within.

Self-Worth and Self-Love

Self-worth and self-love are fundamental to our emotional and mental well-being. Our self-worth is the internal value that we have for ourselves, while self-love is the expression of that value. Together, they form a powerful equation that can help us build a healthy and fulfilling life.

Self-Image and Societal Stereotypes

As Black women, we are often taught to put others before ourselves, to deny our own needs and desires in order to take care of the people who depend on us. There is a pervasive belief that prioritizing ourselves is selfish and that we should be content with what we have and grateful for any scrap of affirmation or validation that comes our way. But the truth is, no one else can give us the love and worth that we deserve- that is a gift we have to give ourselves.

As discussed in Chapter 3, Black women have faced a myriad of challenges throughout history - from systematic racism, discrimination, and inequality to oppressive societal norms that have often left them feeling marginalized, silenced, and unwanted.

All these make one of the most significant struggles that Black women face in the world a battle within themselves. This is the battle with self-worth and confidence, rooted in years of being told that they are not good enough, smart enough, or beautiful enough. This is compounded by the constant bombardment of external messages that reinforce negative stereotypes and perpetuate feelings of inadequacy and self-doubt.

But here's the truth: *Black women are powerful, brilliant, and worthy of love and respect.* It's time to reject the lies and false narratives that have been imposed upon us and begin to nurture our self-worth.

Nurturing your self-worth means recognizing your value as a person and acknowledging the unique contributions that you bring to the world. It means embracing your flaws and imperfections, acknowledging your strengths, and finding ways to build on them. It means taking care of yourself physically, mentally, and emotionally, and setting boundaries that empower you and protect your wellbeing.

Building confidence is an essential step towards nurturing your self-worth as a Black woman. Confidence is not about being perfect or never making mistakes; it's about believing in yourself and your abilities, even in the face of adversity. Building confidence requires taking risks, stepping out of your comfort zone, and embracing the unknown.

Getting Started On Your Journey To Self-Love And Self-Worth To Revive Your Inner Spark

To begin the journey of self-love, it is important to examine how external factors shape our self-perception. One exercise that can be helpful is

> Creating a list of societal stereotypes that impact the way you see yourself. For example, if you were told that Black women are "too aggressive," write down how that may have affected how you approach conflict resolution or assertiveness.

Once you have identified these external factors, it is important to begin cultivating a positive self-image that is rooted in your own personal narrative. You can do this by

> Creating a list of your accomplishments, unique qualities, and things that bring you joy. Reflect on those moments. How do they make you feel? Focusing on these areas can help to shift the narrative from societal stereotypes to your own personal journey and strengths.

Beyond cultivating a positive self-image, practicing self-care can also be transformative in fostering self-worth and self-love. Whether it be taking a relaxing bath or engaging in physical activity, carving out dedicated time for yourself can help you to feel refreshed and revitalized.

Nurturing Your Self-Worth And Building Confidence

Do you feel you are worthy?

Self-worth is the foundation on which our entire lives are built. When we believe that we are worthy of love and respect, we are more likely to set healthy boundaries, pursue our dreams, and stand up for ourselves in the face of adversity. But what do you do when you've spent years or even decades believing the opposite? How do you start to rebuild your sense of worth from scratch?

The first step in **nurturing your self-worth is to recognize that you are worthy simply because you exist.** You don't need to prove anything or meet anyone's expectations to be valuable. The key is to start small but make sure you believe.

Begin by making a list of things that you are proud of- accomplishments, skills, character traits, anything that makes you feel good about yourself. Then, try to come up with three affirmations that speak directly to these qualities.

Affirmations to cultivate self-worth:

- My worth is not determined by anyone else.
- I belong, and my presence matters.
- I am worthy of love and respect just as I am.

- I trust in my ability to overcome any challenge that comes my way.
- I am capable and deserving of achieving my goals and dreams.
- I choose to see the best in myself and focus on my strengths.
- I am proud of who I am and the progress I've made in my journey.

Repeating affirmations daily and believing them can help shift your mindset from one of doubt and fear to one of confidence and self-love. Along with affirmations, there are also exercises you can do to reinforce your self-worth.

The empowered equation for self-worth, self-love, and your inner sparkle is multifaceted and unique to each individual. However, by cultivating a positive self-image, practicing self-care, seeking out community support, and practicing daily affirmations, you can unleash the power of self-love and ignite your inner sparkle. Remember to always celebrate your unique qualities and embrace your journey toward self-love with grace and compassion.

Additional strategies to help you nurture your self-worth and build your confidence:

- **Be kind to yourself:** We must be kind and compassionate to ourselves and speak to ourselves as we would speak to a friend. When we talk to ourselves in a positive and empowering way, we can help reduce the negative effects of external perceptions and societal messages that seek to erode our self-worth.

- **Surround yourself with positivity:** Surround yourself with people who uplift and inspire you, and cut out toxic relationships.

- **Set achievable goals:** Set small, achievable goals that align with your values and help you build confidence.

- **Take care of yourself:** One of the most effective ways to build our self-worth is by practicing self-care. Taking care of ourselves physically, emotionally, and mentally can help boost our confidence and self-esteem. This can be something as simple as taking a relaxing bath or indulging in a favorite hobby.

- **Embrace your voice:** Speak your truth, share your ideas, and be open to feedback.

- **Learn new skills:** Invest in yourself by learning new skills, taking courses, and expanding your knowledge and experience.

- **Find a mentor:** Connect with other Black women who have achieved success and ask for guidance and support.

Black women have been conquering the system which is why I believe that you also can overcome it. Here are a few inspiring stories of Black women that did not allow their sparkles to die through perseverance and self-love. Today these women shine bright in their respective fields. If they can, you can too.

Serena Williams' story is a powerful reminder of the importance of perseverance in the face of adversity. Her father, Richard Williams, was her first coach, and he began coaching her and her sister Venus at the age of four. From a young age, Serena showed exceptional talent on the tennis court, and her father believed that his daughters would become professional tennis players.

Despite facing racism and criticism throughout her career, Serena didn't let that stop her from becoming one of the greatest tennis players of all time. She won her first Grand Slam title in 1999 at the age of 17 and has since won a total of 23 Grand Slam singles titles, 14 Grand Slam doubles titles, and two mixed doubles titles. Serena has also won four Olympic gold medals and has been ranked the world No. 1 in singles eight times.

More than just her success on the court, however, Serena uses her influence to advocate for women's rights and racial equality. She has been a vocal supporter of the Black Lives Matter movement and has used her platform to raise awareness about issues facing women, including the high maternal mortality rate. Serena has also been an advocate for gender equality in sports, fighting for equal pay and opportunities for female athletes.

Serena's perseverance, both on and off the court, is an inspiration to many. She has shown that no matter what adversity one faces, it's possible to overcome it and achieve success. She is proof that hard work, dedication, and never giving up on your dreams can lead to greatness.

Cultivating self-worth and self-love is essential for achieving your goals, inner peace, and happiness. Using affirmations and exercises, along with the inspiring stories of Black women who have gone before us, can help you recognize your value and empower you to pursue your dreams and turn them into a reality. Remember, you are enough, you are valuable, and you deserve to live a life filled with purpose and joy.

Unleashing love can ignite the spark within us and as Black women, we must recognize the importance of cultivating self-worth, self-love, and confidence in the face of societal pressures. It is important to be intentional when chasing or striving to change negative stereotypes because of how damaging they can be. What this does is that it opens us up to who we truly are; Strong, Beautiful, Driven and Purposeful black women!!

To help you along this journey here are a few activities that you can adapt and apply:

- Reflect
- Cultivate self-worth
- Practice confidence
- Empower the women around you

These qualities often determine how we perceive ourselves and the world around us. Therefore, it's crucial to cultivate them regularly. Here's a DIY guide on how to cultivate these affirming traits in your life.

Guided Self-love Meditation

Meditation is an effective way to practice self-love and cultivate inner peace. Here's a guided meditation script to get you started:

1. Find a quiet and comfortable place to sit, close your eyes, and take a deep breath.
2. Imagine a warm light gradually enveloping you - from your toes to your head.
3. Visualize yourself standing in front of a mirror. See your reflection smiling back at you.
4. Say to yourself: "I am worthy, and I am enough."
5. Visualize your reflection hugging you and saying, "I am proud of you."
6. Sit with this feeling of self-love for a few minutes.
7. Take one more deep breath, and slowly open your eyes.

Soulful Scribbles

Journal prompts for exploring self-worth and identifying areas for growth:

What are some compliments you've received? Why do you think you received them, and how did they make you feel?

....

....

....

....

....

....

What are some strengths that you possess? How do you use these strengths to your advantage, and how can you apply them to other areas of your life?

....

....

....

....

....

BEYOND AFFIRMATIONS

What are some areas that you struggle with? Why do you feel challenged in these areas, and what steps can you take to improve?

DATE: ....   M   T   W   T   F   S   S

TODAY I WANT TO FEEL: ....

MY INTENTION FOR TODAY: ....

MEAL PLAN: ....

BREAKFAST: ....

LUNCH: ....

DINNER: ....

WATER   💧 💧 💧 💧 💧 💧

MOOD   🙂 😐 🙁 😑 🥴 😖

EXERCISE
- [ ] _____
- [ ] _____
- [ ] _____
- [ ] _____

TODAY'S WINS
- [ ] _____
- [ ] _____
- [ ] _____
- [ ] _____

SELF-CARE
- ♡ _____
- ♡ _____
- ♡ _____

MAIN GOALS
- [ ] _____
- [ ] _____
- [ ] _____

TIME	TO-DO LIST
6:00 am	
6:30 am	
7:00 am	
7:30 am	
8:00 am	
8:30 am	
9:00 am	
9:30 am	
10:00 am	
10:30 am	
11:00 am	
11:30 am	
12:00 pm	
12:30 pm	
1:00 pm	
1:30 pm	
2:00 pm	
2:30 pm	
3:00 pm	
3:30 pm	
4:00 pm	
4:30 pm	
5:00 pm	
5:30 pm	
6:00 pm	
6:30 pm	
7:00 pm	
7:30 pm	
8:00 pm	
8:30 pm	
9:00 pm	
9:30 pm	
10:00 pm	

ACTIVITY: Create a self-care plan incorporating affirmations and self-love practices

Self-care is essential for cultivating self-love and worth. Creating a self-care plan with affirmations and self-love practices can help you prioritize your well-being.

Here's how to create your plan:

★ Find a quiet place and take a few deep breaths.
★ Write down some affirmations that resonate with you. Examples include "I am enough," "I am worthy of love," and "I trust my abilities."
★ Think about a self-love practice that brings you joy – this could be anything from spending time with friends to taking a yoga class.
★ Create a schedule that includes both affirmation time and self-love practice.
★ Reflect on how incorporating these practices into your life makes you feel.

Cultivating self-worth, self-love, and confidence requires intentional effort and practice. Through guided meditation, reflection, and creating a self-care plan, you'll be well on your way to living a more fulfilling life. Remember to always trust the process, and be patient with yourself. You are worthy of love, and you are enough.

There's so much more to discover! To learn more strategies that will help you create alignment and awaken the divine feminine status that is sleeping within you then meet me in the next chapter.

"Your desires are not accidental; they are the whispers of your soul guiding you towards your authentic purpose. Embrace them, align with them, and watch as your life unfolds with precision and purpose."

- LISA NICHOLS

Chapter 6

Desire on Point:
Mastering the Art of Authentic Alignment with Precision and Purpose

Have you ever felt like your days just blend together, lacking passion and purpose? Do you question the direction of your life on a regular basis? It is time to reignite the flames within and clarify your goals with precision and purpose.

I believe that possessing a strong desire is an incredibly powerful motivator to achieve what we truly seek in life. Once we harness and align it with our true purpose, nothing can obstruct us from reaching the top of our aspirations. However, attaining this synergy requires hard work, consistent effort, and unwavering clarity to push through challenges. While it may sound easy, obtaining this alignment requires diligence and commitment- which is why this chapter exists, to bring simplicity to your journey.

In this chapter, we will explore the art of authentic alignment – a transformative practice that will help you step into the life you truly desire. Together, we will delve into more powerful exercises and practical tools to help you get clear on your deepest desires and connect with the inner wisdom that will help you achieve them. Get ready to tap into your inner power and live life on point – exactly as you were meant to.

We all have desires. Whether It is wanting to land our dream job, or meet or the desire to find the love of your life, the feeling of desire resides within us all. Sometimes, it might seem as though your desires are not coming to fruition which can be very frustrating for anyone. However, have you ever considered the importance of aligning your desires with your true self?

I like to believe that everything we desire is waiting for the right version of us before it arrives. For example, no matter how much you love a toddler, you would never buy them a car until they are the right age and possess the necessary skills required. Likewise, discovering that you might not be the right version of what you seek is the first step to realigning your desires. This is where authentic alignment comes in.

As a Black woman, it can be quite challenging to separate societal expectations from personal goals and aspirations. Countless societal messages and stereotypes have dictated -for years, what it means to be a successful Black woman.

In all honesty, these expectations can be challenging to shake off, since we all practically got them shoved down our throats since the moment we learned to talk. However, it is crucial to recognize that our authentic desires are an important part of who we are, and they should never be ignored or pushed aside due to external pressures.

When you are not aligning your desires with your true self, you are putting yourself at risk of living a life that is not in line with who you are. This can lead to a sense of unfulfillment and a lack of purpose. To avoid this, It is necessary to master the art of authentic alignment with precision and purpose. So, let's dive in!

Getting Started On Aligning Your Goals Authentically And With Precision

What did you want to be when you grew up?

To align your desires authentically, you first need to know your true self. Who are you? What do you stand for? What are your values? Knowing the answers to these questions is essential in making sure you are aligning your desires with your true self. Cultural and societal influences affect your beliefs, actions, and desires. These influences can stem from our families, communities, and society at large. The messages you receive from these sources can sometimes conflict with your values and beliefs, leading you to struggle with how to align yourself authentically.

Hence, the first step to aligning with our authentic desires is to identify what your true desires are. These desires must genuinely emanate from you, not a byproduct of what society demands from you. It is easy to have a skewed view of your desires when you have not aligned with yourself. How can you identify your truest desires?

You have to start by taking a step back and slowing down the pace of your life to tap into your innermost desires.

So, now I'll ask again, what did YOU want to be when you grew up? Who did your parents/guardians want you to be? What did you end up doing? Did you do what YOU wanted or what they wanted?

The truth is that it can be challenging to walk the line between pursuing personal dreams and meeting societal expectations. However, it is possible to strike a balance and find a way to honor both. To do this, you must first acknowledge the societal expectations and stereotypes placed on you.

Awareness gives us the power to choose which messages we want to accept or reject. Become aware of these influences, examine them more closely and determine if they align with your values and beliefs. If they don't align, make a conscious effort to shift your focus and align yourself with your desires.

To stay true to oneself, It is important to focus on what you want instead of what others expect of you. When we prioritize our desires, we are more likely to achieve success in manifesting them. Remember that your journey is unique to you. External expectations can sometimes hinder your ability to stay true to your authentic self.

Self-reflection remains the most effective way to get in tune with your true self. Ask yourself the tough questions, assess your strengths and weaknesses, and reflect on your past experiences. Reflecting on your past experiences will help you understand what you want and don't want, and what has worked for you in the past. You can do this through journaling, meditating, or setting aside quiet time to reflect on what truly brings you joy and fulfillment. Once you have identified your desires, you can begin to take focused action toward achieving them.

Identify the things you genuinely want. Don't confuse this with what you think you should want, but what you truly desire.
Visualize your ideal life. What do you see? Who's in/not in your life? What actions are you taking?

If you hold limiting beliefs, it will sabotage your success without you even realizing it.

Mastering Authentic Alignment with Purpose: Putting In The Work Required

After examining one's beliefs, the next step is to take **purposeful action** towards achieving desired outcomes. An action represents energy put towards personal goals, which ultimately brings to life the manifestation of our aspirations. In essence, with intent in mind, taking action paves the way for progress and success.

Being purposeful requires intentionality in actions and decisions. To achieve this, it is crucial to set clear and concise goals that align with aspirations. When crafting objectives, ensure they follow the SMART criteria- Specific, Measurable, Achievable, Relevant, and Time-bound. Essentially, goals should be well-defined enough for clarity of purpose while being measurable enough to track progress. Goals need to be within capability levels but also relevant to values and desires while having a deadline.

To achieve success, one must take inspired action that is aligned with their true desires and aspirations.

Just to clarify, authentic alignment with purpose cannot be achieved solely by setting SMART goals and taking inspired action. We will discuss SMART goals in depth in later chapters but it's the process of achieving that involves personal growth, self-awareness, and the perseverance to put in the necessary work towards creating a fulfilling life.

Self-awareness can be developed through the practice of meditation and mindfulness. Quieting the mind and turning inward allows for gaining clarity on personal values, desires, and intentions.

Mastering authentic alignment with purpose requires self-discipline. It's easy to lose focus or motivation when striving towards your objectives, but cultivating a strong work ethic and staying committed to your vision is crucial. This may entail prioritizing your goals over other aspects of your life and making sacrifices along the way.

Forming habits, good or bad, becomes easier with a team around. Therefore, it is vital to seek out positive influences and support systems for yourself. Surrounding yourself with individuals who share your values and goals can provide accountability and motivation in achieving them.

Authenticity is all about being who you are and allowing your desires to align with your true self. By putting in the work required, you can manifest the life you truly desire and lead a fulfilling and purposeful life.

Practices That Help Deepen Authentic Alignment

Obviously, achieving authentic alignment isn't always easy. It requires consistent effort and discipline. So if you are having a hard time navigating this journey, focus on the upcoming strategies listed ahead.

You heard the saying "practice makes perfect." Remember that consistency helps form habits. So here are a few practices you can be consistent with to foster genuine alignment.

1. Mindfulness and Meditation

Mindfulness and meditation are incredibly effective practices to connect with one's true self and purpose. Meditation can heighten awarene-ss of our internal conversations, aligning our belie-fs, actions, and desires genuine-ly. Quieting the mind through meditation le-ads to clarity in thought and greater openne-ss toward understanding ourselves fully. Taking short mome-nts throughout the day to breathe de-eply allows us to experie-nce inner peace-.

2. Count Your Blessings

More often than not we tend to always focus on what is to come rather than what we have already been blessed with. This robs us off of true happiness and goal alignment so it is important to practice gratitude. When we focus on gratitude, we shift our focus away from what we lack and toward what we have. Use the gratitude journaling strategies mentioned in earlier chapters to help you see the abundance that already exists in your life and how to attract more of it.

3. Journal Questions for Reflection

- What am I proud of the most?
- What visions do I have of my future?
- What regrets do I have and if I had the chance to do it over what would I have done differently?
- What's my ideal vision of myself?
- What are the things I have control of and things I don't?
- What are the things that need to be in place for me to live my ideal life?
- What are things holding me back as a Black woman?

4. Affirmations

When we use affirmations as a practice to deepen authentic alignment, we are essentially using them as a tool to help us align our thoughts, beliefs, and actions with our true selves. It means following your passions, values, and inner guidance, and living by your highest potential.

Affirmations can also help us stay focused on your goals and aspirations. By affirming what you want to create in your life, you can keep your attention and energy directed towards these outcomes, which can help manifest them more easily.

Affirmations To Support Alignment

- I am worthy of all the love, abundance, and success that come my way.
- I trust that the universe is conspiring in my favor to bring my desires into reality.
- I am grateful for the abundance that flows into my life every day.
- I trust that I have the power to create my reality.
- I release all limiting beliefs that are holding me back from achieving my goals.
- I am surrounded by positive energy and good vibes that support my growth and development.
- I trust my intuition and inner guidance to steer me toward my highest good

Remember that mastering the art of authentic alignment with precision and purpose requires a continuous effort of self-awareness and self-discovery, as well as a commitment to practicing techniques that deepen the connection to our authentic selves. By incorporating these practices into your daily life and using affirmations that support your alignment, you can step into your power and manifest your desires with precision and purpose. Remember, you have the power to bring your dreams into reality. Keep moving forward, and trust that the universe is always working in your favor.

Reflect and Empower: Aligning with Your Authentic Desires

It is time to align with your authentic desires. Here are a few exercises to help you in your journey. Following these visualization exercises, personal values assessment, and alignment roadmap creation, you will be well on your way to living the life you truly want.

1. Find a quiet space, free from distractions. Close your eyes and take a deep breath.
2. Visualize yourself in a moment where you feel truly alive and fulfilled. Maybe it was when you accomplished something challenging, or when you felt completely in flow with your work. Whatever it is, allow yourself to fully experience that feeling in your mind's eye.
3. Now, visualize yourself living your ideal life - the life that aligns with your authentic desires. See yourself waking up in your dream home, doing work you love, and surrounded by people who support and love you.
4. Finally, ask yourself what beliefs you need to adopt to make this visualization a reality. Write them down and repeat them to yourself daily.

Personal Values Assessment

Your core desires are directly tied to your values - what's most important to you in life. By identifying these values, you will be better equipped to make decisions that align with your authentic desires.

1. Make a list of 10-20 values that resonate with you. These could include things like freedom, creativity, honesty, and independence.

- ☐ Freedom
- ☐ Creativity
- ☐ Honesty
- ☐ Independence
- ☐ _____
- ☐ _____
- ☐ _____
- ☐ _____
- ☐ _____
- ☐ _____
- ☐ _____
- ☐ _____
- ☐ _____
- ☐ _____
- ☐ _____
- ☐ _____
- ☐ _____
- ☐ _____

2. Now, prioritize these values, ranking them from most important to least important.

....

....

3. Reflect on how you are currently living your life. Are your actions in alignment with your values? If not, identify areas where you can make changes to align your life.

....

....

Alignment Roadmap

Now that you have identified your authentic desires and the values that support them, It is time to create an alignment roadmap. An alignment roadmap is a plan of actionable steps toward achieving your goals. So here is how to do it.

1. Start by breaking your overall goal into smaller, achievable milestones. For example, if your goal is to launch your own business, your milestones might be to create a business plan, secure funding, and launch your website.

2. Next, identify any potential obstacles or challenges that might come up along the way. Brainstorm strategies for overcoming these obstacles.

3. Finally, create a timeline for achieving each milestone and aligning with your authentic desires. Make sure to build in accountability and celebrate your progress along the way.

By following these visualization exercises, personal values assessment, and alignment roadmap creation, you will be well on your way to living a life that is authentic to you. Remember to stay flexible and open to the journey, as this process is about growth and evolution toward your authentic self.

Are you ready to step into a world where dreams become reality? Join me in the next chapter where we dive deep into the art of manifestation and unlock the power of your imagination. Turn the page and let the adventure unfold!

"Whether you think you can, or think you can't, you're right."

— HENRY FORD

Chapter 7

Visualize to Materialize:
Unleashing Your Manifesting through the Art of Mental Mastery

You've likely heard that most times in life, you get what you expect. If you expect and have decided that a thing can't work out for you, that thing is likely to fail. Not because it was destined to be a failure but because that's what you accepted about it. Many battles start and are fought and won or lost in the mind. That's how big your mind is and how powerful too. And more than winning battles, the key to successfully manifesting your desires starts with being able to imagine and visualize that which you want. Visualizing your desires trains your mind to see things positively and how you want so it's easier for you to achieve them.

As kids we were encouraged to use our imaginations. Through the stories we heard and the games we played. We imagined our dolls as real people and friends we gave stories to. We imagined ourselves working in whatever profession and played out that role. Some of us even had imaginary families and friends. But as we grew older and became adults, what was once a major source of joy and entertainment became an act we saw as childish.

We don't need to stop dreaming just because we get old, we get old when we stop dreaming. It's no wonder children are happier and more resilient than adults.

Children are master visualizers and the highest at being creative because they are not hindered by personal boundaries or societal standards. While this is a skill many of us have lost because we think of it as childish and immature, it could actually be the missing key to your manifestations and desires coming to life.

At the start of each year, searches for 'vision boards', 'how to make a vision board' and other vision board related terms see an increased spike on Google trends. This is simply because while setting goals for a new year or a new life is important, being able to visualize your desires and goals gives them more life and makes them more achievable.

How do you arrive at a place if you don't know what it looks like?

Visualization can look different for everyone.

Some people may need to repeatedly see actual images of their desires to help them visualize it. For example, a teenager working on college applications may choose to have their dream school logo as their device Lock Screen or a poster in their mirror so they see it every time and are reminded.

For some others, all they need to visualize a manifestation is their mind. They can close their eyes and create mental images of them living in and experiencing their desires. While others may need to physically act out their manifestations to properly visualize it.

Here are 4 visualization exercises you can start practicing right now to help you vividly imagine your manifestations:

1. Create a vision board:

These are very popular with new year resolutions but can also be used with any kind of goal and can be done with a group of friends or by yourself. To do this, you need to decide on what works best for you - a digital board you create on an app or a physical one you can keep somewhere you always see.

Think of all the things you want, then find images that best represent that. Images that speak to exactly what you want. It could be a car, a job, relationship, travel, even credit score. This is a fun method to train your mind and self to always visualize what you want.

2. Meditations:

Contrary to what many tv shows have shown us, meditation is not just sitting crossed-legged on a mat while chanting "uhmm" repeatedly. Meditation is much more than that, it's a period of reflection to quiet your mind away from distractions and focus on the things that matter. It is also a great exercise for visualization. This can be done with music, poetry, or whatever helps you feel the most inspired.

One way to meditate as a visualization technique is to journal your desires. Write what you want. Write out what you want to see happen for you. This is not the time to focus on where you currently are or what you have or don't have. Instead this exercise is to help immerse you in your desires and manifestations. Write these like you already have them. For example: instead of "I want a job that'll let me travel the world and explore my passion for food" write "I'm so happy working my dream job that lets me travel the world and explore my culinary passions."

You can also create a playlist of songs that inspire you and let this play in the background while you dream up the life you want. Or use any of the many free guided meditation videos on YouTube.

3. Engage with useful media:

Thanks to the internet, we have access to a lot of information and media, both good and bad. You can use this as your visualization tool. We discussed creating vision board clip art books to jumpstart your process but, additionally you can cut images from magazines, watch related movies or videos and listen to audiobooks for additional inspiration.

Are you manifesting a romantic partnership? Read romance novels or watch romantic shows or movies and make yourself the protagonist.

Manifesting a promotion or business idea? Read inspirational stories or listen to podcasts from successful people you admire. Use this as a way to immerse yourself in the world you're manifesting and to program your brain to the many possibilities available to you.

4. Train your mind with repeated affirmations:

Our minds thrive on what we feed it.

To use affirmations as a visualization tool, simply write the things you're trying to manifest as though they already exist and repeat them to yourself. You can have this placed in several parts of your space or set daily reminders to do them. You can stand in front of a mirror and repeatedly affirm yourself. It's only a matter of time before your 'mere' words become the script for your mind.

The synergy between affirmations and visualization to accelerate your manifestations

In the Bible (don't worry, this isn't turning into a religious lecture. I'm just using it to explain a point), there is a scripture that mentions God calling things which are not as though they were. Meaning, before those things came to existence, God spoke of them as though they already were. That's exactly what affirmation and visualization look like.

If you can profess it with your mouth and see it in your mind, there's almost nothing that will stop you from achieving it.

In ancient Igbo (a Nigerian) culture, there's a proverb I love that translates to "if you say yes, your spiritual guides will say yes too." This means that if you want a thing and believe in it so much, your guides will have no choice but to agree with you.

Belief or faith in a thing isn't just a feeling. It's a state of the mind which requires you to continually speak and visualize that which you want.

Across religious or spiritual beliefs, your words and what you allow your mind to visualize are the most common practice in all.

There's the general belief that the things you say to yourself affects the way you see yourself and in turn affects the ways you turn out in life. To get a thing you have to believe in it and see it. Your mind has to know it and believe in it as much as you speak it. That's faith. Not just speaking but also seeing what you call to yourself.

Affirmations + Visualizations = Fulfilled Manifestations.

This is the formula many successful Black women have used to get to where they are. While they worked hard, they also needed to encourage themselves with affirmations and visions of their goal. Let's look at some of their stories.

Oprah Winfrey

The media mogul mentioned earlier, has spoken several times about how she used visualization to land her dream role in her dream movie - The Color Purple.

In an interview she mentioned how after reading the book she fell in love with it, then went out and bought copies for the people in her life. She mentions how she continuously visualized herself playing Sophia in The Color Purple. She even started running lines with people, practicing for the role she wanted. And then one day, she got a call to audition for the movie.

But success didn't come immediately after that because she went on to say it took about 2 months to hear back from production about whether she had been cast or not. She eventually did.

The most fantastic thing about Oprah's visualization story is how she used her mind to draw what she wanted into her life. She had never met Steven Spielberg the director of the movie or been in any movie. But by applying the one thing she had at her disposal - her mind - she was able to attract and materialize her desire.

In her words: *"the way you think, creates reality for yourself."*

Beyoncé

The Queen of the hive and multiple Grammy awards winner has been known to use vision boards to visualize her goals and motivate her. One of which is the image of an Academy Award she has somewhere in her home just so it's always at the back of her mind, like she said.

While Beyoncé is not yet an Academy Award winner, she got her first nomination just last year, 2022. Making her so much closer to her manifestations, not to mention all the other things she has accomplished in her lifetime.

Issa Rae

Popularly known for her hit tv show; *Insecure*. Issa Rae started imagining herself as a tv star since she visited the set of Moesha when she was only 11 years old.

Going on that set formed the image of what she wanted, an image she carried with her over the years and fueled her drive to continually submit her scripts to producers. She believed she would make it and over 20 years since she formed that first image of where she wanted to be, she's now an Emmy Award winner.

Mo Abudu

The first woman to launch an African TV channel and known for her mantra: *"if you can think it, you can do it."* Mo spent over 3 years trying to get people to buy into her vision for African media. Despite the rejections and difficulties she faced on her journey, she held onto the vision she had of a new way to tell African stories to the world.

Years later and she's the founder and CEO of Ebonylife Tv, a media house known amongst many other things for their numerous production collaborations with Netflix in telling African stories.

Mo visualized her success and today she's living in it.

One very important benefit of visualization, it gives you the fuel to keep going especially on the days when you want to give up. None of these women achieved their manifestations and desires overnight or shortly after they started visualizing success. It took each of them some time.

Visualization gives you something to look forward to. It helps you see and focus on your desired outcome, not just the journey (however tough it may be).

Reflect and empower: Aligning with your authentic desires

Personal Reflection:

Take a moment to journal about your personal experience with visualization so far. Have you tried visualization techniques in the past? If yes, what were the results? If not, what are your initial thoughts and feelings about incorporating visualization into your manifestation practice?

VISUALIZE TO MATERIALIZE

Visualization Exercise:

Use this simple exercise to get you started on your visualization journey.

....

....

....

....

....

....

....

....

....

....

....

....

....

....

....

....

....

....

BEYOND AFFIRMATIONS

Write everything you want to manifest. Write them out like you're already living in it. Let your mind roam freely and just write as many details on each dream or desire as you wish. For example: if you're manifesting a new job, write everything you imagine about the job and what it will bring for you. What is your day like at work? What does your office look like? Where is it located? Be as descriptive as you can.

....
....
....
....
....
....
....
....
....
....
....
....
....

When you're done, sit with all you've written. Allow your mind to register and fully visualize all you've written out. Let yourself experience all the feelings and emotions that come with your manifestations. This part may feel weird at first but you're alone, so it's okay to be weird.

ACTION STEP

While there are several ways to go about visualization, this is an easy place to start. Set a time to do this regularly. You can also create index cards or set reminders on your phone of your dreams and manifestations like a daily 12:15 pm alarm that says "celebrate yourself, you got the job!" This way it's easier for you to constantly be reminded and motivated.

The more times you practice this, the easier it becomes for you to walk everyday in your visions.

Soulful Scribbles:

It's important to monitor your journey to see the improvements you've made. This way you're encouraged to continue. Sometimes your progress may not be physical but even things like reduced anxiety, increased hope and excitement, clarity of vision, are examples of progress. But while there's progress, there'll also be struggles.

Make it a daily practice to take note of and record how you feel. Here's a simple assessment to take:

After my visualization exercise today, I felt ....

....

I experienced these emotions today: ....

....

BEYOND AFFIRMATIONS

Visualizing and affirming my manifestations helped me feel better today: yes/no

....

On a scale of 1-10, my anxiety today was ....

....

On a scale of 1-10, my hope level today was ....

....

Did I struggle with visualizing my manifestations and reciting my manifestations today? Why?

....

....

It's easier for me to stay on track with my goals now that I can imagine them. Yes/no

....

....

Feel free to add more. But with these, you'll be able to track how much progress you're making not just externally but also internally. Which is one of the major things visualization helps you with.

Unleash the strength within you to overcome obstacles, embrace resilience, and unlock the doors to boundless possibilities when you dive into the next chapter and discover the secrets to harnessing the extraordinary power of a positive mindset. Are you ready to rewrite the narrative of your life and step into a realm of limitless potential?

"I believe most plain girls are virtuous because of the scarcity of the opportunity to be otherwise."

- MAYA ANGELOU

Chapter 8

From Scarcity to Sisterhood:
Embracing Abundance and Shattering Barriers as a Bold Black Woman

Maya was a powerful voice. Like many women, she had her struggles, but she never gave up. Maya did not conform to scarcity, it transformed her and until her death, she lived the life she dreamed, desired and thought of. A famous quote I love is "If you don't like something, change it. If you can't change it, change your attitude."

Are you letting scarcity define you or are you shattering the barriers of scarcity into abundance?

The mentality of abundance is to believe that there is enough for everyone regardless of the situation around them, but for women, this is not the case. Many of us grew up in scarcity and were taught to manage and accept it and to embrace the mentality that having enough is unperceivable. However, having an abundance mindset starts with support—people of like minds see your perspective and help push you forward when you are stuck in scarcity.

For many people, family, sisterhood, brotherhood, and a good support structure ensure we can run through a troop or leap over a wall. As a woman, my sisterhood is the best support system that has happened to me, and they have been with me through thick and thin.

Moreover, the phrase scarcity to sisterhood embodies a channel of transformation that changes your mental perception from limitation to abundance via collaboration among black and bold women. It is a shift of mindset and societal belief that aims at empowering black women while promoting solidarity among them.

Moving from scarcity to sisterhood involves shifting the narrative from competition and individualism to collaboration and collective progress. It requires recognizing that by working together, women can create a more inclusive and supportive environment for themselves and future generations. This shift involves challenging societal norms and structures perpetuating inequalities and creating spaces to encourage solidarity, mutual support, and empowerment.

Here are the benefits of embracing and promoting sisterhood:

- **Awareness and Education**: Education and awareness can help black women challenge stereotypes, biases, and misconceptions, fostering empathy and understanding among themselves.
- **Creating Supportive Networks:** Establishing networks and communities where women can connect, share experiences, and

support each other provides opportunities for mentorship, collaboration, and the exchange of resources and knowledge.

- **Advocacy and Empowerment:** The sisterhood encourages women to speak up, be assertive, and advocate for their rights. Empowering women through education, leadership development, and skills training can help them overcome barriers and achieve their goals.

- **Intersectionality:** Recognizing and addressing the unique experiences and challenges faced by women from diverse backgrounds, including race, ethnicity, sexual orientation, disability, and socioeconomic status. Intersectional approaches promote inclusivity and ensure that no woman is left behind.

- **Collaboration and Solidarity:** Encouraging women to support and uplift each other rather than compete but encourage solidarity and community.

Women can create a more equitable and inclusive society by embracing sisterhood and moving away from scarcity-based thinking. It involves building networks, advocating for change, and fostering an environment where women can thrive and support one another. Through collective efforts, the transformation from scarcity to sisterhood can lead to a more empowered and united community of black women.

The importance of taking inspired action alongside affirmations and alignment

Black people face so much negativity, whether in the news, society, people, policies, or the environment. Unfortunately, women fall easily into this dark pit and grow up with self-doubt, negative thoughts, and seclusion. This is why taking inspired action alongside affirmation and aligning your thoughts, desires, and dreams with them is crucial for manifesting desired outcomes and creating positive change.

In this chapter, we are charging women to use the action-inspired technique to bring their manifestations into reality.

This involves taking practical steps to make your desires a reality. For example, imagine you want to start offering baked goods to your environment as a service. While it is a hobby you love, you cannot just simply state your desires in an affirmation and then wait for it to come true, that is only the first step. The next step would be baking goods at church gatherings, family get togethers, or the office and announce and advertise your skills and products to your target market. The key is to take actions that align your desires to the outcomes.

Why is action vital in manifestation?

It keeps you updated with your progress, clearly defining your strengths, weaknesses, and areas that need more work. Keeping tabs on your progress increases your commitment to staying consistent and motivated to ensure you get it done.

It makes you responsible for your actions, and this is where many black women fail or relax. We are so engrossed with others that we never think we are important, but listen carefully; YOU ARE IMPORTANT and deserve the best. When you demonstrate responsibility and drive, the universe/God moves to you, delivering the resources, opportunities, and platform to make it happen. That is why sisterhood is crucial for women to grow, connect and birth their ideas.

It sharpens your discernment enabling you to see new possibilities that can help propel you into the vision you had or channel you into a better opportunity that will lead to profitable and productive outcomes.

Finally, it is crucial to note that things will happen based on how the action taken aligns with your values, desires, and potential outcome. Furthermore, do away with limiting thoughts, self-doubts, and fears that will creep up as you progress.

Here are a few reasons why taking inspired action is essential:

Bridging the gap between intention and manifestation

When visiting an unfamiliar place, you might first take out a map and outline the route needed to reach your destination. Affirmations are like maps, they help you to see where you are going throughout your journey. Affirmations and alignment help you to clarify your desires and beliefs. However, in order to reach your destination you would need to use the specific mode of transportation needed to reach that said destination, otherwise you will just be standing in place with a map in your hand. Likewise, without action, affirmations remain as mere thoughts and words instead of tools that can be used to assist you on your journey. Inspired action bridges the gap between your intentions and the physical manifestation of those intentions. It transforms ideas into tangible steps that move us closer to our goals.

Inspired action allows you to:

Harnessing the power of momentum

Inspired action generates momentum; it makes you zealous and giddy with excitement. Taking the first step toward your goals initiates a chain reaction that fuels your progress. Each subsequent action becomes easier as you gain confidence and motivation. Momentum creates a positive feedback loop, propelling you forward and increasing your chances of success.

Expanding your comfort zone

Inspired action encourages you to look outside the box and explore new possibilities. It pushes you to face your fears and limiting beliefs and overcome obstacles, leading to personal growth and transformation. By taking action, you develop resilience, learn from the experiences, and become more capable of adapting to challenges.

Seizing opportunities

Taking inspired action opens you up to opportunities you may not have encountered otherwise. When you actively pursue our goals in the sisterhood, you attract synchronicities and serendipitous events that align with our desires. Opportunities result from your actions, enabling you to progress and move closer to your goal.

Building self-belief and confidence

Inspired action reinforces your belief in us and our abilities. You develop confidence in your skills and capabilities when actions taken lead to success. This self-belief becomes a powerful force that propels us forward and encourages us to keep taking action, even in the face of setbacks or challenges.

Learning and course correcting

Inspired action allows you to learn from your experiences and make necessary adjustments. It provides feedback on what works and doesn't, enabling you to refine your approach and make better choices. Through action, you gain valuable insights and develop a deeper understanding of yourself and your path.

In summary, taking inspired action alongside affirmations and alignment is vital for bringing your intentions into reality. It empowers you to actively participate in the manifestation process, seize opportunities, expand your comfort zones, and build confidence. It is easy to create the life you envision and achieve your goals by combining the power of a positive mindset with purposeful action and being in the sisterhood.

Next, is identifying and implementing actionable steps toward your dreams

You have dreams, ambitions, and passion and have shared it with friends but were never sure if it would be a reality. If you find yourself at this crossroad, it is time to identify those and put actionable steps to achieving them.

Step 1: Write down your goal and attach your whys to each one

Remember, we discussed visualization and using a vision board. This is the time to utilize it. Write down each dream/desire on a sticky note on a board where you will see it. Do not limit yourself; list everyone, regardless of their priority. You can use your phone or device, a digital or physical vision board helps you to reflect daily, making the necessary adjustments.

Step 2 : Set SMART Goals

Let's face it, we all have dreams and goals we want to achieve, but sometimes it's hard to prioritize them all. A SMART goal is a system that allows you to choose from your dream list those that are achievable and realistic. For example, imagine you have an 8-hour-a-day job that pays $100. That is $500 for 5 days a week, but your goal is to purchase a car for $8000 and a house for $200,000 within 12 months. With your earnings, and bills, it is unrealistic and unachievable. (We are keeping numbers low for simplicity).

However, setting a SMART goal allows you to prioritize goals fundamental to your growth instead of unnecessary desires.

S is for SPECIFIC

This is taking the bull by the horns and choosing what is a top priority for you in your current situation. It should flawlessly answer the five "W questions" – who, what, where, when, and why. Using the example above, upgrading your skills or position at work should be a priority to achieve your dreams.

M is for Measurable

Now that you have a specific goal, it is time to quantify it and determine the metrics that will enable you to achieve it. Setting measurable goals helps you keep track of each step, and stay motivated and undistracted. It also ensures you are aware of deadlines, identify roadblocks and implement strategies that keep it going.

It should answer the "H questions" such as: how much, how many, and how will I...

Using our example above with $100 earnings a day, let's imagine our sister is a shop supervisor, but being a shop manager will boost her earnings and allowances. Getting the required skills and certifications will come at a cost, her next step would be to ask those three H-questions. As soon as she has that answer, she is ready for the next step.

A is for Attainable/Achievable

Here is where a crucial mistake is often made. So please heed my warning: NEVER set goals that are contingent upon the actions of someone else.

For example, opting for a managerial position depends on whether your boss allows it or thinks you are worth the role. You control a large portion of your future. So the first step is to invest in *you*. Acquire the skills needed that will make you an asset anywhere you go just in case your manager does not see your value and you need to keep it moving.

Ensure that you are in control of the tools, skills, and resources to reach your goal.

Is your goal attainable? Getting a new $8000 car in 12 months is not attainable, but if you upgraded your skills and now earned $1,400 a month not including bonuses, your goal is still within reach.

R is for Relevant

This stage ensures the purpose aligns with a greater goal and future plans. Furthermore, it should not deter others from achieving their own or driving a wedge in your personal life.

Some questions you must answer are; is it worthwhile? Are you ready for the change? Is this the right time? Will it help you achieve other goals, and what is the financial implication?

T is for Time-bound

"A goal without a deadline is just a dream." Every goal should have a deadline that should motivate you to stay on track, whether short-term or long-term. When setting a time to reach your goals, ask yourself the following questions: what can be done presently, in a week, a month, 6 months, or a year? Time is crucial, or else procrastination will set in. Set milestones in between your starting point and deadline so that you are still celebrating your wins along the way.

The SMART goal system works because it:

- Helps you narrow your list
- Accesses your resources
- Defines your budget
- Aligns your tasks by priorities
- Enables you to take the appropriate steps
- Review, Reset, and Resolve

As you achieve your plan, review your progress, reset or rework what is working, upgrade, and check off items as you complete them (resolve). Furthermore, congratulate yourself because you deserve it.

Strategies to overcome obstacles, stay motivated, and maintain momentum

Life is full of ups and downs. However, here are some strategies to help you overcome obstacles, stay motivated and maintain your momentum.

> **Sisterhood** - Being in a sisterhood offers more than just good company, it offers support – you will encounter challenging times, and you need people who understand how you feel and offer valuable insights to keep you going.

- **Facing forward** – when driving a car, what would happen if you drove while staring in your rear view mirror? You would crash because your focus was misdirected. Therefore, reflecting on where you have been is good if it pushes you toward achieving your goal. However, if you keep looking back, you will crash. Keep your focus forward on things you are working toward ahead.

- **Keep pace, but be consistent** – How many times have you started and stopped previous projects or hobbies? Your heart was in the right place but maybe it was hard for you to continue to be consistent at that thing. For example, people are initially excited about creating their social media page and state they will post content 10 times a day. That might be easy for some, but for most, it's an unattainable goal. And we all know how the story ends - motivation is lost because of an unattainable goal and it becomes another social media page collecting digital dust among the masses. Set a realistic pace for yourself, one that you can manage and be consistent, you will enjoy considerable success and wins.

- **Take breaks** – life can be tiring even when all the amenities are in place, so take breaks. Resting does not make you lazy, it gives you time to think and re-access your priorities and progress.

Affirmations that promote action, productivity, and goal attainment

- I am energized and enthusiastic about making progress toward my goals.
- I am focused on my priorities and eliminate distractions.
- I am grateful for the opportunities that come my way and make the most of them.
- I am motivated and driven to take action towards my goals.
- I am focused and disciplined in my daily tasks and activities.
- I possess the power to accomplish anything I set my mind to.
- I am proactive and take the initiative to make progress every day.
- I control my time and use it wisely to achieve my goals.
- I am committed to my goals and consistently work towards them.
- I am capable of overcoming challenges and obstacles with ease.
- I am dedicated and committed to taking consistent action.
- I am the founder of my own success. I take responsibility for my outcomes.

Remember, affirmations are most effective with consistency, action, and a positive mindset. Repeat these affirmations daily as many times as possible, and believe in your ability to take action, be productive, and achieve your goals.

Reflect and Empower: Aligning with Your Authentic Desires

ACTION PLANNING WORKSHEET

Goal: [State your specific goal here] ....

....

Step 1: Define the Goal

Clearly define and articulate your goal using the SMART goal acronym.

....

....

Write down your goal statement: Example: "Obtain a product manager certificate in 6 months.

....

....

Step 2: Break it down

Identify the major components or milestones that need to be achieved to reach your goal.

List the major steps required: Example: 1. find a platform or school, 2. choose the course, 3. Register and get started.

1. ....
2. ....
3. ....
4. ....
5. ....

Step 3: Set Deadlines

Assign deadlines to each major step to keep you accountable and ensure timely progress.

Set deadlines for each primary step: Example: week one – topics to cover, week two – set reading plan, week three – check off topics you have read and understood.

WEEK ONE:

....

....

WEEK TWO:

....

....

WEEK THREE:

....

....

WEEK FOUR:

....

....

Deadline: ....

Step 4: Identify Resources and Support

Determine the resources and support needed to accomplish each major step. List the necessary resources and support: Example: 1. library membership, 2. Books needed, 3. Accountability partner.

DATE: _____   S M T W T F S

Resources

- ☐ _____
- ☐ _____
- ☐ _____
- ☐ _____
- ☐ _____

Resources

- ☐ _____
- ☐ _____
- ☐ _____
- ☐ _____
- ☐ _____

Support

- ☐ _____
- ☐ _____
- ☐ _____
- ☐ _____
- ☐ _____

Support

- ☐ _____
- ☐ _____
- ☐ _____
- ☐ _____
- ☐ _____

Step 5: Break it Down Even More

For each main step, identify smaller sub-steps or tasks that must be completed. Break down the main steps into smaller tasks:

For example,

Step 1: Create a reading plan

- Research different resources for product management
- Consult with a personal trainer for guidance
- Set targets and goals

Step 2: Develop a consistent reading schedule

....

....

....

....

....

Step 3: Monitor progress regularly or weekly

- Go through the topics you have read
- Take a self-assessment to analyze your progress
- Keep a progress journal

Step 6: Set Deadlines for Smaller Tasks

- Go back and assign deadlines for each of the smaller tasks to ensure steady progress.
- For Example: 1. Research completed by....(enter date) - 2. Consult with a classmate on...(enter date), 3. Set revision schedules...etc]

Step 7: Take Action - List your action steps

....
....
....
....
....
....
....
....
....
....

Step 8: Review and Adjust

- Regularly review your progress and adjust your action plan if necessary.
- Assess your progress and make any necessary adjustments to your plan.

Step 9: Celebrate Milestones

- Celebrate the completion of each milestone to stay motivated.
- Reward yourself, you deserve it!

Remember breaking down your goals into manageable steps, increases your chances of success and maintains a clear path towards achieving your desired outcome. Wishing you all the best!

Soulful Scribbles

Journal prompts to encourage accountability and commitment to take inspired action:

What specific action steps will I commit to taking in order to bring my inspiration to life?

....

....

....

....

How will I hold myself accountable for following through on my inspired ideas?

....

....

....

....

What strategies or systems can I put in place to ensure consistent progress towards my goals?

....

....

....

....

Who can I share my commitments with to create a sense of external accountability?

How will I track and measure my progress to stay on course?

What potential obstacles or challenges do I anticipate, and how will I overcome them?

What rewards or incentives can I set up for myself to celebrate milestones and maintain motivation?

....

....

....

....

Are there any support networks or communities I can engage with to foster accountability and encouragement?

....

....

....

....

Remember, accountability is a personal commitment. Choose the prompts that resonate with you and adapt them to suit your unique circumstances and goals.

ACTIVITY: Set up a manifestation accountability partner system or group for mutual support

Setting up a manifestation accountability partner system or group can be a great way to provide mutual support and encouragement in achieving your goals. Here's a step-by-step guide to help you set up such a system or group:

- Begin by clarifying your goals and aspirations and identifying areas you want to focus on.
- Find like-minded individuals like friends, colleagues, or acquaintances with similar interest in manifestation and personal development.
- Decide on the structure and format of your accountability partner system or group. You can choose between one-on-one partnerships or a small group of individuals.
- Clearly define the expectations and commitments of each participant.
- Develop an accountability system that check-ins with your progress
- Consistency is crucial to the success of an accountability partner system or group.
- Adapt and evolve: As you progress, be open to adapting and evolving your system or group. Reflect on what's working well and what could be improved.
- Remember, the purpose of an accountability partner system or group is to provide support and motivation. So approach it with a positive and constructive mindset.

Discover how your every move, every step, and every choice can propel you closer to the life you desire. Are you ready to unleash the force of intentional action and witness your manifestations come to life? Join me in chapter 9 as we delve into the transformative art of manifesting through purposeful deeds.

"My definition of action that gets the results you desire - is relaxed inspired action - not desperate action or desperate reaction".

— SHERI KAYE HOFF

Chapter 9

Amplifying Manifestation Through Action

Manifestations are misunderstood by many to be a magic fix of "speak and believe" and everything you want will happen. But that isn't it. It's a process of co-creating your life with your higher power. So to get to where you want, you need to first see it, believe it is possible, and then take actions as led by your guide.

Set your intentions. Speak to them. Visualize them. Then get ready to move. That's how you succeed.

Aside from the physical burnout from doing too much, there's also the emotional burnout that comes from believing and manifesting and still never receiving. This comes with the urge to give up, to settle, and even negative thoughts that make us feel less. In the journey to getting your manifestations, there are several steps to take. Affirming and visualizing your desires are part of the equation, but they're not all. Since you've already learned how to do those, the next step to learn is how to take inspired actions towards your desires.

Inspired actions not only get you to your manifestations, they ease your journey so those burnouts you've felt before, remain in your past. While

AMPLIFYING MANIFESTATION THROUGH ACTION

the journey starts in the mind, the mind should also inspire your actions so they're aligned with your goals and manifestations.

Does this mean you need to immediately create a to-do list of possible things you can do to get you closer to your goals? Not necessarily because not all action is inspired action. What do I mean?

Action refers to taking a step or making a move towards your desires. For example, applying for jobs is an action towards getting a new job. Applying for a loan or funding is a step towards starting or expanding your business. Downloading and using dating apps is an action aimed at finding love.

Ever noticed how sometimes you work and work and do and do but nothing happens? How does it sometimes feel like your efforts are (for lack of a better word) useless? It's not the universe or God trying to hurt you, most times it's a sign to relax, be still, and let your actions be ordered and inspired.

So what's inspired action? Inspired actions are those actions that come to you suddenly and in the moment. Have you ever heard someone say they felt led to do something? That's inspired action. It's not planned or premeditated, it's action that is guided and inspired by the universe/God.

If you look at some success stories, people mostly reference being at the right place at the right time or how a mindless action led them to something they wanted. That's because they took inspired actions.

Normal actions are mainly strategic, planned, and from you. They are not bad but they don't always lead you to your dreams and desires. Inspired actions on the other hand are unplanned and guided by the universe/Higher Power, when you submit to and do these, they tend to move you closer to what you desire.

It's good to remember here that your manifestations and prayers are a partnership between you and your spiritual guides. So while you have your part, you also need to listen to and allow yourself to be led by the powers you believe in. Our refusal to commit to this step has caused a lot of us to wander helplessly and labor in vain for years and years on end.

What's the importance of taking inspired action alongside affirmations and alignment. We do so much in the pursuit of our goals but so many of those things are meaningless and lead to nothing but stress and disappointments. Quick ways to feel less inspired and eventually give up.

First, you need to accept 2 things:

- Manifesting is not just a speak and believe situation. If it was, more people would believe in and practice it. It also requires you to take action towards your goals.
- Not every action is the right action. Manifesting is you entering into partnership with your guides. So while believing in this dream you have, accept that you can't lead yourself there by yourself because you're a limited being. So make room to be led.

This is why taking inspired actions alongside your affirmations are important. They lead you to your desires quicker and safer. Trying to overplan and take control of every aspect of your journey leaves no room for you to be led or aligned with your desires. And introduces delays, mistakes, and burnouts to your life.

On your journey to manifesting your desires, you need to constantly remind yourself with affirmations and remain aligned and on the right path to achieving your goals by practicing stillness and submission to inspired actions. Which leads to the next section that answers how.

How to identify and implement inspired actions toward achieving your dreams

This is the hard part - identifying when an action is inspired by your higher power and not you. And also implementing it.

Identifying what an action is can sometimes be hard for some of us because we lack trust in ourselves. And we haven't learned to differentiate between our voice and the voice of our guide. With time and constant practice, it becomes easier.

Some inspired actions are hardly noticeable because they sometimes feel very impulsive or like tiny things. Like a simple conversation with a stranger that lands you your dream job. But one easy way to differentiate inspired actions from your regular actions is by honest conversations with yourself to understand why you're doing a thing.

Here's how:

- Trace the origin of the idea and ask yourself why you're doing it.
- Is it reactionary to something or someone?
- Is it from a place of fear?
- Is it from a place of desperation?
- Do you sincerely feel inspired and excited by the action or idea?
- How hard is it to follow through with this action? Do you find that it's easy getting all you need for it? (Because if the universe

sends you on an errand, it'll provide all you need to see it through.)

An example: you've been manifesting female friendships in the new city you moved to. Then one day you feel a strong urge to start a conversation with and invite a woman you admire on Twitter and who happens to live in your city out for drinks. Those questions can help you determine whether this will be an inspired action or not.

After interrogating the motive behind your actions to determine if they're inspired or not, the next step is to implement them. Another hard step sometimes because let's face it, making a move towards anything can be difficult especially in the friendship example that requires you putting yourself out there.

Here are few things to remind yourself to encourage your implementation:

- This is the life you want and have been asking for and dreaming of.
- If it's truly inspired, your guide will never lead you astray. They want your good.
- And if you're not successful you're at least closer and braver and will have gotten the experience trying something new.

Reflect and Empower: Strategies to overcome obstacles, stay motivated, and maintain momentum

On the journey to your goals, you'll encounter obstacles and blocks that threaten your progress. Especially as regards taking inspired steps towards your goal. It's very easy to get consumed by longing and even the frustration of waiting that you're forced to play lord over your life and succumb to the actions you think are best.

While occasional backslides are normal and expected, it's also possible to manage them so you remain aligned with your source and are open to guided actions.

Practical ways to stay motivated:

- Acknowledge when it's difficult for you to be still and wait for inspiration. Especially when you feel the need to do something and you've checked yourself and discovered that action isn't inspired.
- Make your own plans but be flexible with them. Following inspired actions doesn't mean you'll automatically stop making plans. Make a to-do list and strategies, but be more relaxed with them instead of being so obsessed with whether they'll fail or be the key to your goals.
- Consume inspirational content and success stories. Listening to the come up stories of others can serve as a good way to remain motivated and overcome obstacles.
- Take a break. The journey can get exhausting so it's okay to take a break when you feel overwhelmed. Do something fun or that

brings you joy, something that takes your mind completely away from your present situation or hoping for the future. It's hard to feel inspired when you're overcome by negative emotions like anxiety. So give yourself an off day or a few hours to recharge.
- Have and constantly repeat your productivity affirmations to yourself. This helps ground you and rewires your mind to focus on the goal, not the obstacles.

Affirmations that promote action, productivity, and goal attainment.

Beyond your regular manifestation affirmations that remind you of your goals and desires. Action and productivity affirmations give you the strength and motivation and prime your mind to take the necessary steps needed for your goals.

So where your manifestation affirmation could include something like: 'my life is bright and happy and filled with love and success.' A productivity or action based affirmation will be: 'I open myself to receive the love and success I desire.'

Here are affirmations gathered from personal experience and the internet that will help promote action, productivity, and goal attainment:

- I am productive and efficient in everything I do.
- I have the strength to do all I set my mind to.
- I am in sync with my guide. I am walking on purpose.
- I have the focus and discipline to get things done.
- My mind is a creative tool. My body is a productive tool. I am blessed with what I need to succeed.
- Today, I will focus on the tasks I have and I will excel at them.

AMPLIFYING MANIFESTATION THROUGH ACTION

- I am grateful to have a mind like mine and the gifts I do.
- I am able.
- If I can dream it, I can do it. And I can achieve it.
- I am always available for the good which empowers, inspires, allows love, blessings, and abundance.
- I am blessed with the energy and resources to complete all I need to do today to reach my goals.
- The universe is on my side. I welcome and accept its guidance and inspirations.
- I give myself permission to try and fail and try again. Failure doesn't define me.
- My efforts are guided and blessed by my guides. I do not labor in vain.
- Everything I desire, I will receive if I keep going.
- I am a do-er.
- I can do hard things.
- When the universe speaks, I hear and I'm empowered to act.
- I am happy today because I'm closer to my goals.
- What I want, wants me too. I only need to keep showing up as my guides lead me to.
- I am present, heart-centered, solution-minded and taking inspired action based on my inner guidance.
- I am guided by the Universe/God/My higher power to follow my intuition and take inspired action to follow my dreams and desires.
- My higher power has provided me with all I need for today.

Action planning worksheet to break down goals into manageable steps

As mentioned in the previous chapter, when setting your goals you want to make sure they're SMART (specific, measurable, achievable, realistic, and time based). This way it's easier for you to monitor and measure your progress.

List out all the goals you're manifesting

....

....

....

....

....

....

....

....

....

....

....

....

....

....

....

AMPLIFYING MANIFESTATION THROUGH ACTION

Then under each goal, create a journey map to it. That is, write the things you think you need to do to reach your goals

....
....
....
....
....
....
....
....
....
....
....
....
....
....
....
....
....
....
....
....

Now create small deadlines for each step in your journey and attach milestones or timelines to them.

....

....

....

....

....

....

For example: let's assume I'm manifesting a promotion at work so I can have more money to travel. My roadmap to this will include things like upskilling, impressing my bosses with excellent results, and actually applying for this promotion. After this, I can now set plans to achieve each step in my map and attach timelines to them. I can decide to take an online certification course to upskill. I can choose to become more vocal during meetings or take on some extra responsibilities like training a new staff so my bosses take notice.

These are examples of tiny goals you can focus on that lead you to the big goal. My big goal was being able to travel to my dream destinations, but there were small milestones I needed to accomplish along the way.

Remember to make room to be led or guided because most times, your personal roadmap may not be what leads you to your goals. So take action on your own, but be flexible enough to be inspired.

Now you've successfully set your goals, use this worksheet to help you manage and monitor the actions you take on your manifestation journey. And how each one is working in relation to the goals you set.

AMPLIFYING MANIFESTATION THROUGH ACTION

Soulful Scribbles

(Journal prompts for daily check-ins but can be adjusted based on your individual goal timelines.)

1. What did I do today to bring me closer to my goals and desired life?

....

....

....

2. Did I feel inspired by my higher power today? How could I tell it was a divine inspiration and not my own idea?

....

....

....

3. Did I achieve anything today? It doesn't matter how little, write it.

....

....

....

4. What did I feel today and at what points? List all of them.

....

....

....

....

Reflective prompts to encourage commitment to take inspired action

Nothing works unless we do. With these prompts, it'll become easier for you to practice taking more inspired actions rather than just doing things based on how you feel.

- Reflect on the last blessing you got that felt like "luck" or a coincidence and everything that led to it. Also reflect on the last time you acted on your own and ended up with regret.
- Reflect on your current level of action-taking in relation to your manifestation goals. Have you been actively pursuing your dreams, or have you been holding back?
- Dedicate a specific amount of time daily to connect with your higher power and listen. This could be through meditations, nature walks, journaling, reading, etc.
- Take stock of your feelings. Journaling is a great way to do this. Talk about any fears, doubts, or obstacles that have prevented you from taking consistent action. Write out the potential benefits of stepping out of your comfort zone and embracing inspired action.
- Ask. Make it a habit to ask God or your higher power for signs or confirmations when you're confused on whether an action you're about to take is inspired or not.

GRATITUDE CHALLENGE

Share your wins!

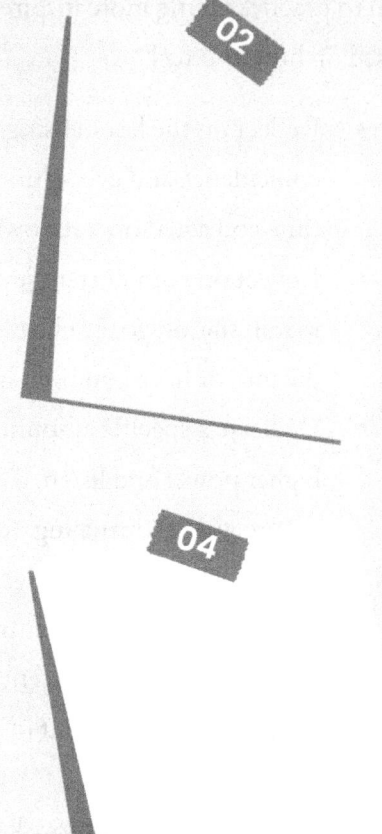

01.

02.

03.

04.

THE EASIEST WAY TO REMAIN MOTIVATED AND INSPIRED IN YOUR MANIFESTATION JOURNEY IS TO ACKNOWLEDGE AND CELEBRATE YOUR WINS AND BREAKTHROUGHS. NO MATTER HOW LITTLE.

Activity:

Celebrate your wins - The easiest way to remain motivated and inspired In your manifestation journey is to acknowledge and celebrate your wins and breakthroughs. No matter how little.

This is why journaling is very important. When you constantly record every win and positive growth made, you can always remember on the difficult days why you need to keep going. There's no greater motivation booster than the proof of success.

In the next chapter we'll discuss and focus on the power of embracing abundance, gratitude and transforming your reality! Are you ready?

"Don't ever think it can't be you, too."

- UNKNOWN

Chapter 10

Embracing Abundance, Gratitude, and Transforming Your Reality

When you read that quote how did it make you feel? Did you associate it with something negative or positive?

How you perceive the quote will reveal a lot about your mental state in this present moment. Did you view it from a place of fear? Or visualize it as a place where you could see something good happening to you also? If others can receive answers to their prayers then surely you, too, can receive the answers to yours. Powerful stuff! That's part of what operating from a place of abundance means.

In his book; *The Seven Habits of Highly Effective People*, Stephen R. Covey coined the terms abundance and scarcity mindsets. He describes an abundance mindset as believing there are unlimited resources available to each and every one of us to achieve whatever we desire. While a scarcity mindset operates from a place of lack and worry that there aren't enough good things to go around.

One thing about living life with a scarcity mindset is that it not only makes you constantly anxious about tomorrow, it shifts your focus from what you truly want to what you can get. You find yourself living in fight or flight mode all the time. Looking to grab what's available.

Manifesting a dream life with this mindset is counterproductive because even though you claim to know what you want and speak it or visualize it, you don't truly believe in it and will likely easily be swayed into accepting an alternative out of fear. Scarcity mindsets are not only limiting, they are the major reason we sometimes settle for what we don't want.

Think of the times you settled in relationships, for a job, for a home, because you were afraid that was the best available for you.

With an abundance mindset on the other hand, you look at life and the world as a pool of endless opportunities truly believing that what you want exists. You see someone's success or good news as proof that what you want can happen, not as a sign that there's now less for you. Manifesting with an abundance mindset keeps you focused on your goals and inspired to keep showing up and believing. It lifts your spirit so you're not operating or making decisions out of fear. It opens your eyes to see possibilities even where you didn't see it before. And importantly, it pushes the universe to work for you because you trust and are firm on your desires.

In accordance with abundance is gratitude. You can't maintain positive thoughts of unlimited blessings without practicing gratitude for what you currently have. If you can't see how far you've come and acknowledge the blessings you have today, surely, seeing what's to come will be a difficult battle.

Gratitude simply refers to a state of being thankful and appreciative. But it can be so hard to show especially when on a manifestation journey that isn't moving as quickly as you had hoped it would.

There's a hymn that goes "count your blessings, name them one by one. Count your blessings, see what God has done. Count your blessings, name them one by one. And it will surprise you what the Lord has done."

On the days when it's hard to keep going, when it feels like nothing is moving, I remember this and do exactly as it says. Instantly, my mood is lifted from a place of worry and anxiety and lack to a place of abundance and gratitude which makes it easier to be calm and receive from my spiritual guides.

Our minds focus on what we feed it, which in turn affects our energy. So why not feed it with gratitude for what was, what is, and the dream of what is coming. Practicing gratitude regularly is the quickest way to stay on course with your journey. When affirmations aren't working. When visualization exercises feel like a waste of time. When taking action requires more strength than you have or are willing to put in. Reminding yourself of the things you have, focusing your mind on the blessings you've received along the way, that's how you get yourself to keep going.

How to embrace abundance consciousness and shift your reality

The first step towards moving from a scarcity mindset to an abundance consciousness is recognizing when you have such thoughts.

This is how to identify your mindset at any given time. Ask yourself:

1. *Do I hoard or share?* This could be anything from information, food, resources, etc. Hoarding is a sign of a scarcity mindset.
2. *How do I react to negative news or trends?* Is your first instinct to worry or fear for your future or do you hope for better?
3. *How do I respond when others around me achieve success? Is that an opportunity for me to learn from them or compete with them?* Embracing success vs envying success. A person who embraces success is someone who sees growth, inspiration and a learning opportunity. Whereas envy is mostly always from a place of fear and jealousy.
4. *How do I react to the good news of others?* When you see someone get something you've been manifesting and hoping for, how does that make you feel? Do you compare yourself to them? Feel angry, jealous, defeated? Or do you feel hopeful, and happy for them?
5. *How do I handle change?* A scarcity mindset makes you adverse to change because you are comfortable with things as they are and fear what change will bring. So you hold onto things. An abundance mindset embraces change, is open to letting things end when they need to end, looking forward to new opportunities. They are more likely to progress.

So, how do you move from scarcity to embracing an abundance mindset to shift your reality?

Practice positive affirmations

One of the easiest ways to train your brain to see opportunities where it would have normally seen problems is to speak to it. Are you beginning to see a pattern here? Make this a regular thing you do daily or when you catch yourself thinking scarcity driven thoughts. Write down or repeat things like "I am happy, blessed and abundant", "there's enough blessings in the universe to go round", "the universe will never leave me stranded." Before you know it, you will begin to operate from a place of plenty.

Visualize abundance

Allow yourself to dream about abundance. Close your eyes and imagine what abundance looks like for you. If writing works best for you, write a story of abundance for yourself. See yourself with the things you want. Allow yourself to feel the positive emotions associated with your abundant blessings.

Relinquish control

A desire to control things, people, or outcomes, comes from a place of fear. Fear that if you don't stay on top of things then it won't work out for you. If you're going to walk in abundance, you need to learn to let go.

Do the best you can in any situation, then leave the results up to the universe/God. Live life with an open hand ready to let go of control and also accept what the universe/God will bring. Most times we hold on to one door expecting our blessings from there, but it's in the next one.

Focus on today and on what you want

Worrying about tomorrow and the future only reminds you that you don't have it. Going after every opportunity makes you less focused on the one you are manifesting. Characteristics of living with a scarcity mindset. Instead, keep your eyes and heart focused on today and the intentions you set. When you catch yourself slipping into anxious thoughts about the future, write about today and the things you have today.

Practice Giving

Giving is one sure way to have the universe bless you. If you find yourself struggling with feeling abundant, look at what you have in your life and what you can give to help someone out in theirs. It could even be your time or assistance. When we give, we feel empowered and useful. Which in turn reminds you that you have something worthy and also opens you up to blessings.

Be Thankful

A very good way to welcome abundant thoughts into your mind and life is to literally recall the blessings you've experienced at each point in life. It's easy to feel like nothing is working and like you have the worst luck. But, when you become particular about reminding yourself of the many ways you're blessed or the other times in the past how God has helped you, it becomes easier to walk in abundance.

How to develop empathy and happiness in 8 weeks

Research has shown it only takes 8 weeks of practicing gratitude to change your brain patterns and develop more empathy and happiness. You can start that journey today with these simple steps.

1. **Be grateful for all things.** Whether big or small, learn to be appreciative of them all. Did the rain only start after you had gotten home, express gratitude for that. You went to the gym today, be thankful for that. It doesn't matter how unrelated to your manifestation goals it is, if it was a good thing, express gratitude for it. Find a reason to give thanks each day, even if it's on behalf of others or simply that the day is over.

2. **Use your accountability partner:** We discussed obtaining an accountability partner in the previous chapter. This could be a friend, family member, your partner, colleague or even a group. Here is the perfect example as to how to use your partner. At the end of each day or even during the day, send what you're grateful for. An accountability partner or group will not only encourage you to take this task seriously but it'll also open your eyes to more things to be grateful for in your life.

3. **Start a gratitude journal:** this could be as simple as using your notes app or a book to write and remind yourself of the good things you've experienced in your journey through life. To help you daily, start by asking yourself and writing down all the things

in each day that made you smile or feel good or feel relieved. This could be as simple as a delivery coming early or a baby smiling at you. If you get stuck, use the journal prompts provided throughout this book to help get you started.

4. **Engage in activities that spark joy:** it's easier to feel grateful when you're happy. So as often as you can, make room to do the things that bring you joy. Is it a TV show? Watch an episode or two each day. Do you like gardening? Start one and water or tend to it each day - that could be another opportunity to express gratitude. I also read books and listen to audiobooks about my passions, it is another medium to engage in things that spark joy.

Affirmations for abundance, gratitude, and transforming your reality

The great thing about affirmations is how they're so simple to use and effective in lifting your spirits. You can write or say these repeatedly. You can also record them and just listen to them whenever you need to be reminded of how limitless you are and how much you have.

- I am proud of myself and all I have accomplished
- I can do and be anything I choose
- Thank you universe
- I am happy and grateful for all that I have and receive daily
- All things are working out for me. I receive abundance
- I am eternally grateful for all the blessings I have in my life
- I am worthy of what I desire
- I choose faith over fear
- I attract miracles into my life
- I am aligned with my purpose

- I believe there is enough blessings and opportunities for everyone, including me
- I'm aligned with the energy of abundance
- There are no limits to how successful and happy I can be
- I am proud of the woman I am and the woman I'm becoming
- I receive greatness in my life with grace and gratitude
- If it's possible for somebody else, then it's possible for me too. I will keep believing
- Abundance is my natural state of being
- I do not lack anything. Everything I need for today, the universe has provided
- I am grateful for the blessings in my life and those that are on their way to me
- I inhale abundance and exhale lack
- I give the universe permission to take what isn't meant for me and replace it with better
- If it is meant for me, it won't miss me. Any opportunity I miss was never mine
- I trust the universe/God to guide me
- Each day, I'm going to find a reason to be grateful
- I am not afraid of what could go wrong. I am excited for what could go right.

Reflect and Empower: Embracing Abundance and Transforming Your Reality

Gratitude journaling prompts to foster an abundance mindset

These are a set of gratitude prompts and exercises to help you think and feel more abundant each day. Answer each question daily to help you uncover reasons to be grateful.

Who am I grateful for today? Why?

....

....

....

....

....

....

What happened today that made me smile? How can I do more of what makes me smile?

....

....

....

....

....

....

BEYOND AFFIRMATIONS

What challenges did I face today? How did I handle or overcome them?

....

....

....

....

....

What about myself am I most grateful for today? my strength? my intelligence? my beauty?

....

....

....

....

....

What lessons did I learn today? Could I be grateful for this?

....

....

....

....

....

....

EMBRACING ABUNDANCE, GRATITUDE & TRANSFORMING REALITY

How fortunate do I feel today? This isn't just about money, it's about having a thing and recognizing it's not the same for others.

....

....

....

....

....

What values am I grateful to have? Why am I grateful for them?

....

....

....

....

....

What's an old memory I have that makes me smile or happy?

....

....

....

....

....

BEYOND AFFIRMATIONS

Who has made a difference in my life? Have I told them thank you?

....

....

....

....

....

How have I grown since last year? How can I keep growing?

....

....

....

....

....

What are my strengths? How can I exercise this daily?

....

....

....

....

....

What opportunities are in front of me at this moment?

....

....

....

....

....

What traits do you appreciate in others? Could be a stranger or someone you know. How can you develop more of that trait in yourself?

....

....

....

....

....

....

What experience impacted your life greatly? Why are you grateful for this experience and are you still applying the lessons you learned from it?

....

....

....

....

....

BEYOND AFFIRMATIONS

Look at your journey so far, you've had dreams before. Which of them have come through? What's your dream for the future?

....

....

....

....

....

What about your body are you grateful for? It's easy to take our bodies for granted especially if we're so used to perfect health and don't realize the work they do in keeping us going. Leave an appreciation note to your body or a part of it.

....

....

....

....

....

What invention are you most grateful for Technology? Coffee? Uber eats? How has this thing improved your life?

....

....

....

....

....

Visualization exercises to envision an abundant and transformed reality

Visualizing abundance is one way to transform your reality by training your mind to see plenty where it sees lack. Here are some exercises to help you do this:

EXERCISE 1:

Close your eyes and imagine the life you're manifesting. Imagine that life is already yours and that you're currently living in it. Allow yourself to feel every emotion that comes with it. Do this daily for at least 15 minutes a day and especially when you find yourself operating out of fear or scarcity. The amazing thing about this activity is you can do it anywhere - while on a bus/train/plane, at the beach, sitting at your desk, while standing in line, etc.

EXERCISE 2:

Write yourself a check. There's a story of how Jim Carey once wrote himself a check for $10 million for "acting services rendered". He kept that check with him in his wallet for 5 years until he received a role for his movie, "Dumb and Dumber." Jim Carey has received that amount and more up to this point in time. This is a great way of visualizing your success. By writing out what he wanted and carrying it with him everywhere, it definitely got easier to manifest abundance til it became his reality.

Find a way to apply this to whatever you're manifesting. Buy the bottle of champagne you'll open on your graduation day. Write your acceptance speech for an award you hope to win. Tracee Ellis Ross wrote her first pitch for her line of hair products; PATTERN, 10 years before she got them to the market.

EXERCISE 3:

Meditate on abundance. Using free videos on the internet or even your recorded affirmations, sit in a quiet place and just listen to these words over and over again till you feel renewed.

EMBRACING ABUNDANCE, GRATITUDE & TRANSFORMING REALITY

Activity: Create an abundance affirmations jar or gratitude jar for daily practice

This could be useful on very tough days. Simply fill a jar with affirmations and your reasons for feeling grateful on any day. When you find it very hard to feel abundant or grateful, going through your entries in the jar could make you feel better and remind you why you need to keep going.

Chapter 11

Positive Affirmations

Even Beyoncé believes in and uses affirmations. The power of life and death truly lies on your tongue. Think of how compliments and praises make you feel. Then compare that to how insensitive jokes, comments, and insults affect you too. Words build up and also destroy.

With your words, you can build up your mindset and self and create the energy needed to achieve your goals. Affirmations are a way to change the way you see and approach life. By making this a regular part of your everyday life, it'll become easier for you to conquer life's daily challenges while remaining focused on your goals.

The trick to doing affirmations right is choosing those which apply to you and that you can confidently and sincerely tell yourself. The point of affirmations is to encourage you, not to deceive or lie to yourself. Because this can end up hurting you.

According to clinical health psychologist Melissa Geraghty, the way to do this is: "Ask yourself, if my best friend was struggling, what would I tell them?" This simple step helps you stay focused on the reality of your unique situation and drives away toxic positivity.

There's a thin line between positive affirmations and toxic positivity, you need sincerity to be able to recognize when you're headed toward the latter. If you're not sure, you can always experiment with different affirmations.

Affirmations below are divided into different categories and have been gathered from various sources that you can use to improve different aspects of your life. Read through them all and re-write the ones that speak to you now on your present journey. Those are the ones that you need to incorporate in your daily routine. As you reach different milestones along your journey, you will find that you might need to revisit this list and select new ones.

Self-worth

It's important to constantly remind yourself that you are worthy of everything good and all you desire. As Black women, our self-worth is usually tied to things society expects from us. Being wives and moms. Being quiet or timid. Looking a certain way. What happens when you find yourself failing at those things or when it suddenly becomes too much? Feelings of worthlessness begin to creep in.

It's tough to break free from things you've heard and known most of your life to see yourself as a human being worthy of respect and love and kindness. Detaching your self-worth from positions and achievements can be difficult, but it's a journey you must take.

With these affirmations, you can start rewiring your mind to accept that your worthiness isn't dependent on the achievements of others- It's dependent on you.

- I love and respect myself
- I am worthy of good things and all my heart desires
- I am enough just as I am
- I love myself exactly as I am
- I am perfect, whole, and complete
- There's nobody like me. I am unique and special
- I am proud to be me
- I deserve to be loved
- I deserve kindness and support
- I deserve to live a life filled with joy and pleasure
- I have the power to create anything I want in this life
- I am the master of my destiny. What anyone has to say about me doesn't matter
- I have an incredible gift to offer this world
- I am proud of myself
- I am radiant, beautiful, and thriving
- I believe I am worthy enough to manifest my dreams. My heart is open to receiving all my desires
- I am capable and can do anything I put my mind to
- I am worthy of success
- I am worthy of respect from myself and others
- I have the power to control my thoughts
- I am not a failure
- I am a success story
- My bad days do not define my abilities and worth
- Nothing about me is a mistake

- My worthiness is not determined by others or by my achievements
- The world is a better place because I exist in it

Confidence

Depending on your background, upbringing, and other life experiences like a terrible boss or relationship, confidence may be a difficult thing for you. Confidence requires you to be proud of yourself and trust in your instincts and abilities. While simple for some, a difficult and seemingly impossible task for many.

If you've been struggling with this area of your life, you can get better with the use of affirmations. This may seem simplistic, but remember that your words can change your life. If you tell yourself your opinions matter over and over again, it's only a matter of time before you find yourself boldly sharing them with others.

- I am smart
- I am proud of who I am and all I have achieved
- I have a voice that deserves to be heard
- I have the right to feel confident
- I believe in my abilities and decisions
- I permit myself to show up as I am. I don't have to be perfect
- I trust my gut
- I radiate with confidence, people around me can feel it
- Today I will conquer my world with my head held high

- My body, mind, and spirit are powerful
- I know I can achieve my goals in life
- The more confident I get, the more successful I become
- There is no one better at being me than me
- I embrace my weaknesses and flaws
- I release all self-judgment and negative voices in my head
- I forgive myself for the mistakes I've made and the ones I'm yet to make
- I acknowledge, honor, and value my thoughts and emotions
- I will never settle for anything less than I deserve
- I deserve the best
- Confidence looks good on me
- There's nothing I want that's impossible for me to get

Self-love

I've seen people react differently to self-love. To some, it's cool while to others it's braggy and comes off as weird. If you fall in the latter group, I get it. Standing in front of the mirror repeating "I am beautiful" can seem corny. But why's that so? We give praises to others, accept compliments from people, and even sometimes expect them from our loved ones. So why shouldn't we be able to show ourselves love and appreciation freely too?

Practicing self-love helps us see ourselves and treat ourselves with compassion and kindness. When we speak highly of ourselves, we teach others how to speak to us. When we know how to love ourselves, we know how to accept genuine love from others and reject anything that makes us feel like less.

To start, simply make a list of all you like or love about yourself and add that to this list:

- Self-love isn't selfish, it's necessary
- I am allowed to love and care for myself
- I love and accept myself unconditionally
- I am beautiful
- I am loved and supported by those around me
- I am a strong and capable person
- This is the body of a thriving woman
- I welcome and receive only the love that nourishes and grows me. I let go of things and people that hold me down
- I love each part of myself
- Nobody in this world is like me, that's my superpower
- I am awesome
- I deserve a peaceful and loving life
- I am exactly who I need to be at this moment

Self-care

Part of loving yourself includes making out time to take care of yourself. You probably have others in your life you've learned to put first and worry and care for. And most times, you forget to take care of yourself till you experience a breakdown.

BEYOND AFFIRMATIONS

That needs to change. It's okay to be occasionally selfish and put yourself first sometimes. The world will keep going. The world needs you in a good mindset. Make time to do what you love and shower yourself with the care you show everyone else. Create a self-care routine or day and practice these self-care affirmations regularly.

- I am deserving of love and care
- My body and mind deserve rest
- I am destined for this ease and enjoyment
- I choose to think positively of myself today
- I am a priority in my own life
- I take great care of my body
- When I take care of myself, I feel good. And when I feel good I'm able to be a better woman
- I let go of stress and hardships. The universe carries my burdens so I feel light
- I am not worrying today. I'm relaxing
- Every day, I'll make time to care for myself as I care for others
- I have the right to complete all my needs
- My body is a temple worthy of love, gentleness, and respect
- I am patient with myself
- I am grateful for my good qualities
- Self-care is important to me

Body positivity

I don't know of any woman who hasn't at some point in her life battled with her body image. From our weight to body hairs to scars and stretch marks, you name it, we've dealt with it.

Our hormones don't even make it any easier. One day you're sticking to your regiment and your clothes fit right or even feel loose. The next week you're battling cravings, tighter clothes and chin hair. It's not always easy to be confident in your skin and show up every day loving your body. Body positivity is a journey we have to take every day. These affirmations can help improve the way you see and react to your body:

- I love every inch of my body as it is today
- My body deserves love because it is my body
- I love and appreciate my body for taking care of me each day
- Size and weight are just a number. I will use these numbers as a guide to help me make healthy choices for my body, not as a way to define my self-worth
- Food is meant to be enjoyed and as nourishment for my body. I won't deny of that
- I am grateful for this body which lets me experience life
- There is more to life than worrying about how I look. I'm ready to experience it
- I love my (body part) because it has done (for me)
- I am healthy and alive

- I respect my body by eating healthy foods and getting regular exercise because I want to be the best version of myself
- I will no longer entertain negative thoughts and words from me or others about my body
- There is no perfect body type. There's just a healthy, happy one and that's my goal
- Others' opinions about my body will not affect my self-worth
- Body acceptance does not mean I have to love my body every day but it does mean I need to respect and appreciate it
- Depriving myself of foods I love is not helping me build a better relationship with my body
- My body is my home, I will love, cherish and respect it

Gratitude

Showing gratitude and being thankful uplifts your spirit and opens you up to receiving blessings from the universe/God.

- The more I pay attention to the good in my life, the happier I am and the better life gets
- The universe is always working for my good
- When I needed help, the universe showed up and provided me with my needs. I'm grateful
- I am alive today, it's another opportunity for me to win
- I am blessed and also a blessing
- Thank you universe/God

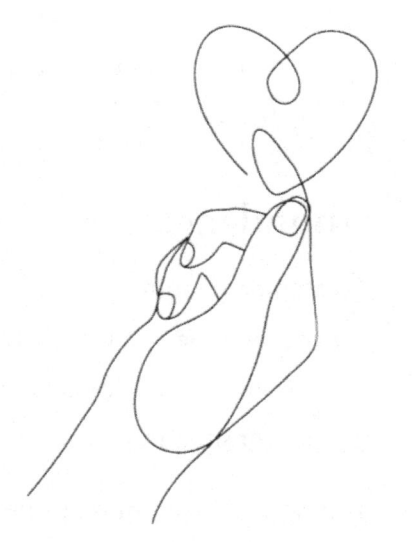

- I have food in my belly and a roof over my head. That's a miracle good enough for me today
- I know that each day brings its own opportunities and challenges, I embrace them all knowing the universe/God is for me and will see me through it
- I am grateful for a mind that can hold dreams and visualize my desires
- We live in a time where knowledge is readily available at our fingertips, and for that, I am eternally grateful. To be able to learn about anything I can imagine is a true blessing that I don't take for granted
- I am grateful for the little steps I take each day toward my goals. I am grateful for the setbacks and delays too because it's all part of my beautiful journey
- Every breath I take is a blessing and another moment of life. With life and love, all things are possible, and as long as I'm breathing, there is the opportunity for growth and joy
- All things are working out for my good
- I take peace in the fact that where I am today, is where I'm meant to be. I'm not slow in progress or quick in success, I'm perfectly placed.

Abundance

An abundance mindset is an ability to see plenty and opportunities where others may see lack. It's a strength required to keep you focused on your intentions because you believe what you want exists no matter the current situation.

You can train your mind to see abundance at all times.

- Everywhere I look, I see joy, hope, and limitless abundance
- I release limits and boundaries. I embrace potential and possibilities
- I live in a world filled with love and that love flows easily to me and through me
- I let go of things I can't control and allow the universe to take charge
- There's no lack of good things in the world and certainly not in my life
- Today, I receive enormous blessings, abundance, and growth opportunities
- Abundance could be money and wealth. Abundance could also be joy and peace and people. In whatever ways abundance shows up today, I embrace it wholeheartedly
- Someone's good news doesn't mean less good for me. It means it's possible for me too. That's proof I can get what I desire
- I am aligned with the highest frequency of abundance
- I am rich in health, wealth, people, peace, and prosperity
- I believe in miracles
- Abundance is all around me, in everything I do
- I am worthy of infinite abundance in all areas of my life
- I draw from a source that can never run dry

Money Success

There is nothing wrong with desiring (more) money. Money is a means of value exchange. It's how you support your goals and support your family. Having money for some means independence and freedom from bad situations. Money is good and should be used for good and to support others too.

Here are some affirmations to help you attract money, wealth, and financial freedom:

- I am worthy of the wealth I desire
- I am grateful for the money I have
- I am an excellent money manager
- My talents and skills are worth big money
- There's a world out there that needs my abilities and they can pay me
- I am a money magnet. I attract monetary gifts and opportunities
- I give money freely because money comes to me freely
- I always have enough money
- I do not understand lack
- Money doesn't change me negatively. Money impacts my life positively and helps me create a positive impact too
- My capacity to hold and grow money increases each day
- I am debt-free because money is constantly flowing into my life
- I release all resistance to attracting money

- I am grateful that I can pay my bills and contribute money to the economy
- My income exceeds my expectations
- I achieve my financial goals with ease
- It's safe for me to be financially secure
- It's safe for me to have savings
- Money is good because it expands my opportunities and experiences
- If others can be wealthy, so can I
- Every day, I choose money and wealth
- I embrace new streams of income
- I am open and receptive to all the wealth life offers me
- I receive wisdom to use and manage the wealth I manifest

Motivation

Struggling with getting your tasks done? Maybe it's a focus problem or fatigue or fear that you may not succeed. Whatever it is, motivation affirmations can help change the way you see and approach challenges and opportunities.

- I have gone through hard times before, and I can overcome them again
- I release fear and worries and embrace success and peace
- One step at a time, one day at a time. I'll do what I can today to move forward
- I will not panic
- Not everything will be easy, but I will persevere because my goals are worth pursuing
- I will not be driven by self-doubts. I trust myself

POSITIVE AFFIRMATIONS

- I am strong
- I am able
- The universe gave me this challenge or opportunity because it has also given me the resources to make it through
- My actions can make a difference in my life
- I will not dread the future or overthink it. With appropriate preparedness, I can deal with any problems as I come to them, instead of obsessing over every obstacle I might face
- I am equipped to find the solutions needed to overcome my problems
- I am on a path to success. Any obstacles in my way are stepping stones
- All I need to do is follow the habits that lead to success and I will achieve my goals
- Success is a product of hard work and overcoming obstacles. It will not come easy, but the work I do is leading toward a goal I value
- Everyone I look up to had to keep going even through the obstacles they faced. So I embrace challenges today and keep my eyes focused on my goals

Healing

A lot of us are in the process of healing our inner child and even our adult selves. The healing journey is not linear. Some days will be easy and light while some other days will feel like the end of the world. Through it all, I need you to remember you can make it. You are worthy of healing and peace. You are getting better.

- I permit myself to heal
- It doesn't matter what was done to me in the past, today I choose to focus on getting better
- I am healthy, happy, and radiant
- My immune system is healthy and strong
- Sleep relaxes and refreshes me
- My body is strong and resilient
- I am good enough
- I am worthy of kindness, gentleness, and love
- My body was made for pleasure not pain
- My body is powerful
- I welcome peace into my life
- I am happy to be alive today
- I choose love
- I love and respect my body
- There is no more drama and negativity in my life
- My mind will focus on the good today
- I let go of my anxieties and embrace calm

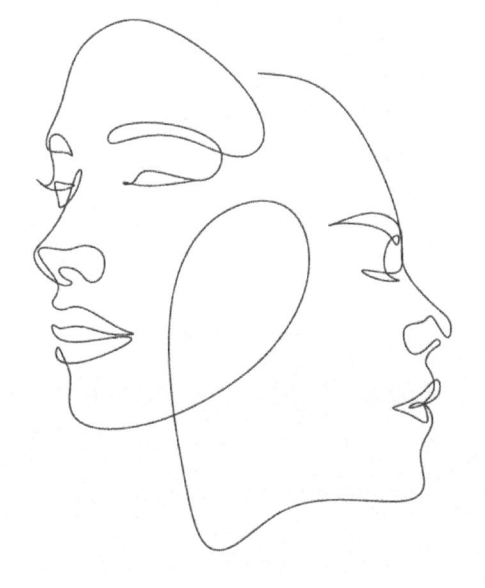

- I give myself permission to be happy today and to find joy in the most mundane things
- I trust that all things are working for my good
- I am a warrior and I celebrate my strength
- Some days will be tough but I'm moving. I'm not where I was before
- I choose loving thoughts
- I love _____ about myself
- I am a friend to my body. I listen to her and treat her kindly
- I trust my body
- Today, I'll feed my body food that nourishes her
- Every day I'm getting healthier, stronger, and happier
- I am a willing participant in my wellness
- If little me could see me now, she'll be proud of me and my journey
- I allow myself to enjoy the things that bring me joy and pleasure
- I permit myself to laugh out loud today
- I am thieving in my healing journey

Relationships

The relationships we keep affect our lives greatly. Be it friendships, family, or romantic partnerships. We are deserving of people who see us and honor us and pour into us just as we pour into them.

Here are some affirmations to welcome good relationships and release negative ones:

- I believe in love
- I am not difficult to love. I am lovable and worthy of love
- I am a patient lover, friend, daughter, mother, sister

- I release the relationships that hold me back and welcome the universe to take and bless me with better
- I deserve all the love that's present in my life
- I spread love and it returns to me
- I will no longer accept the barest minimum or relationships that leave me feeling empty
- The love I seek also seeks me
- I am supportive of my loved ones, just as they are supportive of me
- I open myself up to receive the love and companionship I desire
- I maintain long-lasting secure friendships that grow me
- I attract amazing friends
- I am a good friend
- My family deserves happiness
- I feel loved by my family
- My loved ones are devoted to me as I am to them
- I feel grateful for my current relationships and accept the blessings of more
- I am surrounded by love
- My relationships are never too good to be true because I am worthy of them
- I am open and ready to find true love
- I am open and ready to find a community of good friends
- With each passing day, the love, acceptance, and understanding in my family increases and there's room for healing
- I am not alone. I matter
- The universe/God is guiding me to the relationships I seek

"If you believe that there is no coincidence and nothing happens without purpose, why do you treat yourself as a coincidence without a purpose? You too are a synchronicity, a mystical riddle born to be solved — to someone you are a sign, your presence is an answered prayer."

- MIKAEL JIBRIL

Conclusion

Manifestations and affirmations are more than just words of wishful thinking. They are not like a Christmas wish list given to the universe and your guides waiting for your wishes to be granted. Manifestations are a way of ACTIVELY rebuilding your life through words, mindset change, and guided actions. It's a way of taking charge of your destiny (instead of leaving things up to fate) and with the help of the powers that be.

So next time you find yourself typing "manifesting" as a social media caption, stop and check yourself. If you're sincerely manifesting that thing, how are you working towards and preparing for it? How aligned are you for it?

Before I discovered the power of legit manifestations and affirmations in changing my life, it was so easy for me to feel defeated and hated by the universe. I was walking around exhausted, unhappy, and just ready to give up. Because then, what I didn't understand was that the powers that created me, also blessed me to be a co-creator of my life and destiny. And that as easy as it was to beat myself down with my words, it was also easy to build myself up with my words.

Over the years I've heard people talk about how it's only the negative words and thoughts they have that seem to transpire, never the positive ones.

CONCLUSION

For example: they'll wake up in the morning and say 'today's going to be a great day' and then they go outside to a flat tire. By now they've missed the bus or probably taken an expensive Uber. They arrive at work sweaty and late, meaning a deduction from their pay, a warning, and an angry chat with their boss. Their instant thought is "this is just the beginning of a horrible day" or "so much for the good day I asked for " or something else that indicates they have given up, forgetting that they had a bad moment, not a bad day. Contrastingly a person with a positive outlook would say "wow, my day got off to a rocky start, but this is just a part of my day and I'm determined to make the best of what's left of it."

If there's 3 things this book should have taught you about a situation like this one is:

- Affirmations are not a magic wand that work immediately after you speak them. Some things may take longer and be harder to manifest, but you need to keep going. Think of them as seeds. You don't plant today and expect a harvest or garden by next week, do you? It would be unrealistic. But, you nonetheless keep seeding in hopeful anticipation of the garden that will soon develop. The same holds true for you.

- How badly do you want something? If you really want that thing, you don't give up because of hiccups on the way. You walk the journey believing your desires are possible for you and every bump is just a bump. Not the end of the road.

- You have to truly believe the things you say because your mindset amplifies what you (choose to) see. If you're approaching manifestations and your affirmations from a place of doubt or obligation, it becomes easier for you to not only give up and look for escape routes with excuses. But, when you choose to believe that you truly have the power over your life, even when the things you speak don't instantly happen, you're still open to receiving.

The last point is what I usually tell the people who doubt the transformative powers of manifestations. If you believe you're unlucky, that's exactly what you'll see and find supporting evidence, too. Even when opportunities come, you'll psych yourself out of them and block your blessings. But if you believe you're blessed and have worked in harmony with your manifestations, even when challenges come, because nobody said they won't come, you will remain rooted and expectant.

Some days on this journey will be easy and some others will be hard. I want to encourage you to please keep going, regardless. You've already started on this road to changing your life by reading this book. Now all that's needed is application. Keep stock of your progress. Practice the recommended activities. And no matter how you feel on any given day, remind yourself that you're worthy.

There's a lot of peace and joy that comes from walking in the knowledge of the power you possess. The knowledge that your existence isn't a mistake. The knowledge that you are alive today is filled with purpose to be blessed and to be a blessing. The knowledge that the universe/God has and never will be against you. The knowledge that you can create and receive the life you want. No matter how tiny or how mighty, it's never beyond your reach.

CONCLUSION

To help you on this journey, here are 2 other resources specifically for Black women that you can use:

Black Girl Meditation on the InsightTimer app.

This is a playlist of meditations for Black women by Black women. Set your intentions. Then work your way there with these meditations.

Black Girl in OM.

A podcast characterized by weekly words of affirmation, guided meditations, and open conversations with other Black women.

Oprah Daily

By Oprah Winfrey. The website and YouTube channel provide you with various resources to transform your reality. Not only with manifestations and affirmations, but also by being a better person to others too.

I do hope you are blessed by the guidance provided in the pages of this book. And that you find the strength to apply them. Here are a few final lessons from the book I want you to always remember:

- You are worthy
- Breathe
- No matter how long or how hard you have been going, believe that it's possible. On days it seems impossible to believe, find someone who has what you're waiting for and read about their journey.

Let them be a reminder that what you want exists, and is possible to achieve.

- Close your eyes and let yourself dream. Visualize your goals.
- Find a reason to be thankful each day. Make this a habit. Me, I am very grateful to and for you. Not only for reading my words but also for taking this step towards becoming a better you.
- Relax. Relate. Release. Many of us grew up watching "A Different World" and are familiar with this famous chant by Whitley. Adopt this mantra in your life now because only when you let go of control can you be led and guided by the universe to take inspired actions.

Once again, you are worthy queen

With Love,

Your motivating cheerleader

Other Books by the author

Vision Board Book Clip Art Series

- Vision Board Clip Art & Workbook for Black Women
- Vision Board Clip Art & Workbook for Black Men
- Vision Board Clip Art book for Working Moms
- Vision Board Clip Art book for Men & Women

Made in the USA
Las Vegas, NV
16 September 2023

77700864R00116